My Heart *ROCKS* for Christ

D1739187

Donna Sprague

ISBN-13: 9781079768497

Printed in the United States of America

DEDICATION

To my husband, Bill,
who demonstrates and reflects
the love of Christ every day.

Thank you for always believing in me
and cheering me on for the completion
of this book.
I couldn't have done it without you.

I love your heart and I cherish you.

ACKNOWLEDGMENTS

I am forever grateful for the dedication and expertise of my Christian editor, Craig Bourne. Thank you for guiding me along this journey with your insights and suggestions, and for being my sounding board. I appreciate all the hours you spent reading and rereading my manuscript, and editing my book with the flow and message I wanted to convey to the reader. All your efforts have made this book possible and I deeply appreciate you.

Heartfelt thanks to my photographer, Michael Milliken, who spent hours taking photos of the special stones that grace these pages. Thank you for your gift and talent of photography in capturing the essence and beauty that God has created.

I thank each of my entire family, who have loved me my whole life, from the bottom of my heart, for your endless love and encouragement as I traveled the peaks and valleys of my life, and for always being there. I love you all, and I have the joy, knowing we will be together forever one day in Heaven.

To Mary Ann Olsen, who was first my landlady, and then became my sister in Christ. I will be forever indebted to you for sharing your deep love of Christ with me, even when I fought it and didn't want to hear it!

With heartfelt gratitude to my church family at Presbyterian Church of the Master in Mission Viejo, California, and First Presbyterian Church of Littleton in Littleton, Colorado. You all had an enormous impact on my life and played a vital role in growing my faith in Christ to a deeper level. I am so blessed and thankful to each one of you.

I am deeply honored to have had Rev. Dr. Vicki C. Orr as my mentor when I was a new Christian and taking my first baby steps. She took me under the shelter of her wings and guided me in so many ways on what it meant to be a Christian, always with grace and love. I know my prayer life is what it is today because of this one-of-a-kind godly woman.

And most importantly, I stand in awe of my Lord and Savior, Jesus Christ, knowing He is the giver of life, both here on earth and forever in Heaven. To Him be the glory now and forevermore, for I know, truly, the best is yet to come.

And I hope all who read my book will know it, too.

CONTENTS

Preface

Let me begin by explaining the title of this book, because it has a double meaning that wraps up my whole story.

If you're not familiar with the slang expression of 'rock', let's take a moment with that. When someone says, *"You rock"*, it is kind of like saying, *"You're awesome"*, or *"You're really cool."* It can also mean, *"I like you a lot and I admire you."* A person might say, *"You rock my world,"* which would be a very high compliment. That would certainly be an accurate, though very informal, way of expressing how I feel about Jesus Christ.

And then, as you will read, I have gotten very swept up by finding rocks that are shaped like little hearts, and I have shared them with countless people as a way of sharing the love of Christ. We might hyphenate the word and call them heart-rocks.

So, you see, what I'm saying in the title is that I share my heart-rocks with people because Christ rocks my world. They are a very simple, practical way of sharing His love with the world.

Here is an example of how that works:

> I was the Deacon at our church in California and ministered to the Home-bounds—those who are unable to come to church. One day our church secretary called and asked if I could make a special visit to a woman whose daughter in Colorado had just moved with her

husband to our community. Shortly after their move, her daughter was diagnosed with leukemia. This brokenhearted mother was asking if anyone could pay a visit to her daughter to offer prayer and hope.

So I grabbed my Bible and a heart-rock and off I went. I remember her name was Debbie. She and her husband had moved to California to follow their dream of opening a restaurant. She was going through chemo and then would have a stem cell transplant. We exchanged phone numbers and I told her she could call me anytime.

I will never forget the day Debbie called me at work. She was in the hospital at City of Hope and wanted to let me know her stem cell transplant was taking place. I could hear a lot of activity around her with nurses talking and asked specifically when it would happen, because I wanted to be praying for her.

She said, *"It's happening right now, right this minute. The cells are being transfused into my body and I'm holding my heart-rock in my hand, and I know God is with me and I'm going to be ok."* Tears immediately welled up in my eyes; I was moved and blessed to know God had used me to bring comfort into her life during a very traumatic event.

Her transplant was successful and she and her husband moved to San Diego to open their restaurant. Unfortunately, we lost contact and I never heard from her again. But I know, without a doubt, God had used me once again to pour out His love to someone who was hurting.

A couple more examples:

> A few years ago, a friend, who was a member of our church in Littleton, Colorado, told me about her brother-in-law who was dying of ALS, Lou Gehrig's disease. She asked if I would send him a heart-rock, which I did immediately.
>
> A few days later I opened my email to find a message from him. He was thanking me for such a special gift that he said he would treasure always. He told me every morning he would place his heart-rock in the windowsill of his kitchen and let the sun warm it up. Then he would hold the rock in his hands and feel the warmth of God's love melting away the pain and suffering he was feeling.
>
> He included a picture of his hands cradling the rock. Sadly, he passed away before I had the opportunity to meet him in person, but I felt so blessed that I could reach out and comfort him through the gift of a heart-rock, and I thanked God for using me to minister to him.
>
> We lived in beautiful Colorado for eight and one-half years. Early on I discovered an exquisite gift shop located inside a Catholic church, not far from our home. The first time I went in to just browse and check it out, I discovered small organza bags with silver crosses embossed on them with a little drawstring. The perfect thing to hold the small heart-rocks I would pass out to women. They were beautiful and the perfect size to carry in a purse.
>
> I hit it off with the lady who managed the gift shop. (I love people and have never met a stranger.) I told her

about my heart-rocks and how I use them to bless others with the love of Christ. Then I gave her one. She loved it, and she loved my story so much that she told me whenever I needed more little bags, she would sell them to me at a discount, because I was doing it for the glory of God, and it was a ministry of blessing others.

Eventually we moved back to California, but often made road trips back to Colorado to visit our wonderful neighbors and our church family at First Presbyterian Church of Littleton. I always made time to visit the gift shop to restock my supply of the cross organza bags.

During one of our trips out, I went to the gift shop to buy more bags and the lady was so happy to see me. She knew we had moved, as I made it a point to let her know we were going back to California, and reassured her she would see me again.

After hugging and a little bit of small talk, she got tears in her eyes and told me she had lost a very dear friend recently and was really mourning her loss. She told me that one particular day she had been feeling so down and sad, but when she reached into her purse searching for something, she found her little cross bag that held the heart-rock I had given her a few years earlier.

It was at that moment, she told me, that she was comforted by God's love—knowing she could run to the Rock and be safe under the shelter of His arms. And to me, that's what these heart-rocks represent, a tangible reminder that we are NEVER alone as we journey through this chaotic life here on earth. We can carry hope in our hearts because of the gift of Jesus and the sacrifice He made for each one of us. I praise God for all the ways He has brought special people into my life, to share with them what Christ has done for us all.

I do love Jesus! He is my first love. I love Jesus more than anything. And because I wear my faith, as some may express it, 'on my sleeve', many people have asked me if my love and passion for Jesus has always been a solid anchor in my life. The honest answer, the truth without a doubt, is a resounding, "No". Absolutely not!

Before we get to more delightful stories I have about collecting and sharing my heart-rocks, let me tell you how this all came about. The story of where I began my journey on this incredible path.

I Was a Stranger to Jesus.

I didn't know Jesus, I wasn't connected to Jesus and I certainly didn't depend on Jesus for anything. When I look back on my life, I feel so ashamed of how I had always put myself before Him. I always thought I had my life in control and that I could handle anything. I liked doing it my way.

I was the Donna who everyone thought had 'it' together. Or so they thought. But Jesus knew the real me—what a mess I was, how lost I was— and I didn't understand how much He loved and cared for me, His beloved daughter.

Here is a little story that points out how clueless I was:

> The day my daughter, Heather, graduated from San Diego State University in 1992, I was seated way up high in the bleachers, waiting for the ceremony to begin. As the graduates came walking out onto the field, there was one young man in particular who caught my eye. On the top of the mortar board of his graduation cap was written in big, block letters, **John 3:16**. I said to the person seated next to me, *"Hey, see that kid down there, John, with 3:16 on his cap? We*

share the same birthday March 16th...3/16. But why is he advertising his birthday now, when it's the middle of June?"

Well, needless to say, it wasn't too long after this that I discovered, John 3:16 had absolutely nothing to do with John's birthday or mine! Many have said it to be the miniature version of the Bible, the whole Bible in a nutshell. It's been translated into more than 1,100 languages. It tells of One who loved us with an everlasting love.

> For God so loved the world that
> He gave His one and only Son,
> that whoever believes in Him shall
> not perish but have eternal life.
> *John 3:16*

Well, I'm sure God was looking down on me that day saying, *"Oh, Donna, Donna, my beloved child. You are so clueless and you have been so lost. Have I got a surprise for you! Put on your seatbelt and get ready for the ride of your life!"*

It wasn't until I reached a point in my life when everything started to unravel that I realized I couldn't keep the charade up any longer. I never knew Jesus in a personal and intimate way. I never knew, nor could I fathom, how high and how deep His love was for me.

Like so many others, it wasn't until my life was spiraling out of control and I was sinking down into the pit of hopelessness, that the only choice I had was to look 'up'. With God's gentle nudge, instead of running away from Him, I started to walk slowly, taking baby steps towards Him. My choice to become a Christian wasn't something that was earth-shattering or happened overnight. It was a process God had designed just for me, for He knew I was fragile and broken. But this I can tell you. I knew it was something, and it was something big that had been missing in my life for many, many years, and boy, was I ready for a change!

And so Jesus, in His tender and selfless loving way, got a hold of me, the 'lump of clay' that I was, and He placed me on His Potter's wheel. The process had begun, and, believe me, it has not finished yet. Even as I write this, I continue to be a 'work in progress', moment by moment, each and every day. There is always more in store—to learn ways to grow and new ways to fall more deeply in love with Jesus when we walk with Him. But this I know:

He who began a good work in me will be faithful to complete it...
Philippians 1:6

This is my story, but God had already written it.

I found this rock while jogging in Columbia Falls, Montana. I spotted it and took note of a landmark nearby, so that I could drive back and find it again

It is not a heart-shaped rock itself, but appears to have a heart that is custom carved within the stone. Isn't God just the most magnificent designer?

* * * * *

＊ ＊ ＊ ＊ ＊

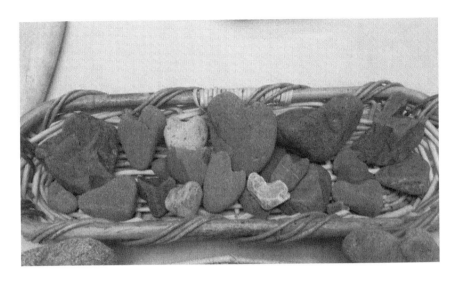

* * * * *

* * * * *

* * * * *

Part 1

Rocks Don't Grow, but I Finally Did!

And by His stripes we are healed.

Isaiah 53:5

~1~

God's Love

I live by faith in the Son of God who loved me
and gave Himself for me.
Galatians 2:20

There are many threads in the tapestry of my story that have all come together to make a marvelous cloth. Follow me as we focus on some of these threads, and watch how they all 'work together for good.' First, let me tell you of my childhood and what an attitude I had in my younger days as an adult!

I was baptized when I was just three weeks old. As a child, I attended Sunday school, and as I got older, church services as well. I knew there was a God, and I knew He had a Son, Jesus, but I never quite understood that whole Trinity thing. And I definitely wasn't walking with Him. Because of my unbelief and insufficient knowledge of the Bible, I was afraid to trust God with my life. Besides, I thought I always did a pretty good job of controlling my life and I liked the way I did it. I thought my life was perfect and it was always my way…the right way. I had no room for, nor did I desire to have God in the life I thought I was running just the right way.

But, instead of feeling happy and content, my life was now consumed with anxiety, worry, nervousness, low self-esteem, and tremendous fears that, in a lot of ways, kept me immobilized and shut off from life itself. I was frustrated and confused. I always thought I was doing everything right. So why did I feel on the inside that everything was so very wrong?

God in all His wisdom knew me inside and out, yet He loved me just the way I was, flaws and all. Even with my sins and my hardened heart that wasn't ready to believe in Him, trust in Him and walk with Him, He still loved and cared for me, because I was His beloved child.

Looking back now, I can't believe the measures I took to be in charge of my life, and of the lives of my family. I tried to be perfect in every way. I thought if I were perfect I would be loved and therefore I'd be happy. But like so many others, it wasn't until my life was out of control, with no way out, facing difficult situations, that I finally turned to Jesus.

My life started to unravel when my marriage of twenty-six years fell apart; my father was dying of cancer; I had undergone surgery that had complications; I received an unexpected job transfer; and my son was choosing the path of drugs. How could everything in my life—my life that I thought was so good at one time—be so drastic and sad now? Remember, I had done it my way, the perfect way—so how could this be?

Suddenly, I could no longer keep the juggling act together. I couldn't keep the balls up in the air anymore, and my world started collapsing all around me. I didn't know where to turn to or where to go. I was going down a deep black hole and I wanted to die. I was filled with hopelessness and despair. I saw no future and no reason to go on. I felt worthless and unloved. I wanted to end the pain.

I know now, without a doubt, that Jesus can take anything that's ugly and evil and turn it into something good and beautiful. The cross brought salvation into the world and when my heart was ready, the cross brought it to me, too. I know my sins are forgiven; they have been blotted out and Jesus remembers them no more. I know Jesus is real, that He died a cruel death, and that He did it for me. I am saved by grace, and

I stand in utter awe of His love. I long to follow Him forever. The cross made the difference to me.

It was through my journey that I came to know and believe Jesus gave up His life for me so that I can live with Him forever in Heaven. The debt has been paid in full. It is not a gift we can buy or barter for. It's through God's amazing love that He gave His Son to pay the price for each of us. The debt has been nailed to the cross. When I think of the horrific pain Jesus endured for me, especially when He was completely innocent of any crime, I feel so undeserving, and yet I know I'm going to Heaven one day. For it is by His stripes that we are healed!

God's in control and only He knows the future, but change can be hard and scary, too. You have to be willing to let go and let God. You have to trust and have the faith of a mustard seed. I wanted to hang on to the way my life had been, because, even though it was not healthy, each day was predictable. Predictable was my normal, comfortable rut that I had been in for so many years.

But remember, I was, and still am, on the Potter's Wheel. Jesus knew my pain, and He would use it to create something beautiful in His perfect time. He was gently bringing me to another level, even when I was fighting it every step of the way. He was preparing me for a life I could never have imagined.

But first, I had much to learn about myself. I would soon be going through the 'refiner's fire'. And in the midst of it all, I began to collect heart-rocks.

~2~

Brokenness

The Lord is close to the
brokenhearted
and those crushed in spirit.
Psalm 34:18

Like many people from my generation, I married very young. My husband and I were only nineteen when we married, but we were in love and couldn't wait to start our lives together. We found a one bedroom apartment, fully furnished, for $95 a month! We thought we had moved into a castle, but worried how we would come up with that rent money each month.

We longed to start a family, and I couldn't wait to be a mother. Three years into our marriage, our daughter, Heather, was born. Seventeen months after that, we welcomed a son, Aaron. We didn't have a lot of money, but we still enjoyed fun adventures with our children, going to the beach and camping. Money was tight, and we cut corners, but I was so thankful I could be a 'stay at home' mom. To me, that was my most important job.

I wanted to be the kind of mother my own mother was to me—always there when we kids came home from school with a fresh batch of cookies cooling on the rack. I wanted to be her, always putting the interests of her kids first and foremost.

My dad was a Marine. There wasn't much money in the Marine Corp, particularly with six kids, but mom always found ways to help bring in a little extra money. She had been blessed with the God-given gift of playing the piano by 'ear', so she often played at the Officer's Club at the El Toro Marine base, and she also did waitressing. With four daughters, she learned how to sew simple shifts for us to wear, and by the time we all were married, mom had become an accomplished seamstress and made all of our wedding gowns. Mom could stretch a pound of hamburger meat and make magnificent dinners that would feed us all. She was a wonderful cook and cooking was another way of showing her love to us. My mother was the epitome of courage. She was industrious, generous, responsible and selfless. She was truly a Proverbs 31 mother. She was my Hero!

So when I had my children, I knew it wasn't about me, or my wants and needs anymore. I had two kids, and I wanted nothing but the best for them. That meant being home when they came home from school, sacrificing and making sure they had a wonderful childhood in every sense of the word. I wanted nothing more than to create and nurture a happy home where my children would have wonderful memories to look back on.

As the years went by and the children were growing up, we kept busy with all the activities kids get involved in: soccer practice, surfing, and drill team, to name a few. I was always the team mom, and I was very active volunteering at their schools and on the PTO. Life seemed pretty good and, in comparison to other families, I thought we were doing a good job. I thought all was well.

But somewhere along the way, my husband and I started drifting apart. Because I wanted the best for my children, perhaps I was putting too much focus on them and not enough on him. I'm not really sure. When a marriage breaks up, I know it's not totally one-sided, but I do know I became lonely in my marriage and I felt like I no longer had a partner. He wasn't there for me, because he couldn't be, at least in the way

I felt a loving and devoted husband should be. I know I was in denial, thinking it really wasn't all that bad at the time, because I wanted my children to grow up in an intact family, not a broken home like I had.

As the years kept going by, one after another, we fell into a pattern where each day was pretty much just like the day before. Things continued to get worse, and I realized I couldn't 'fix' my husband, nor did I have the power to end his need for alcohol. I felt overwhelmed, isolated and confused, and I didn't have a way out. Our kids were still in their teens, and I had no intentions of breaking up our family until they were raised. We lived in a nice home and a beautiful community, and the children had many friends in our neighborhood. I wanted to keep it all together and provide a happy home for our children. And I think I did, for the most part.

During this time frame, our daughter was away at college, and our son would soon be graduating from high school. Finally, it would be 'my' turn. My thoughts and dreams for happiness and well-being were going to be all about *me*— at last!

When the principal at my son's graduation announced his name and placed his diploma in his hands, I looked heavenward and silently said, 'Thank you God', even though God wasn't a part of my life. In a strange kind of way, I felt like I had graduated, too, and would be moving on into an unknown future, but one I was willing to take and not look back.

It was at that moment I knew I would leave my marriage.

Life Is Messy, Isn't It?
We can never plan everything, nor work things out the way we want them to be. I saw a bumper sticker on a car once that said, 'If you want to make God laugh, tell Him your plans'. Or another one was, 'Life is what happens when you're making

other plans'. It just seemed there was always something more serious that took priority in my life. Such is the cycle of life, and I had to rearrange what I wanted to do and place my wants and desires up on a shelf somewhere out of the way, at least for the time being.

About the time my son graduated from high school, my dear father, at the age of sixty five, was diagnosed with colon cancer and given one year to live. I was devastated and brokenhearted to know this sweet man I loved and called Dad would soon be leaving us. How could God take a wonderful man like him away from us?

My dad was actually my step-father, but in every sense of the word father. Kenneth M. Whiteley was indeed my dad. He married my mother, who had four children from a previous marriage under the age of seven. (I have no memory of my biological father ever living with us.) I was the second-born; I had an older brother, Gilbert (Gib), then two younger sisters, Sarah and Jacqueline. Later, when I was an adult, I remember hearing the story of how my mother and my 'dad' met.

My dad was a twenty-nine-year-old soldier, had never married, and was stationed at Camp Pendleton, California, right outside the beach town of San Clemente, where we lived. My mother was a waitress at Woody's Café. The story was that my dad wanted to go out and have a few beers with some of his other Marine buddies, but one of them said, *"No. You have to meet this gal, named Sunny."* My mother's real name was Sarah, but her nickname was Sunny, because of her sunny disposition and smile. So Kenneth Whiteley met my mother; they clicked, fell in love and married within a couple of months. Then we were off to Oahu, Hawaii, where my new dad was being stationed in Kaneohe Bay. I was eight years old.

What fun we had living in Hawaii. Every day was a sunny day, eating mangos, guava, building forts in the vast bamboo forests, and going to school barefooted if we wanted to. We lived just a couple of blocks from the beautiful and warm crystal blue ocean, so that's where we kids played just about every day. Swimming, collecting seashells and building sand castles.

We would collect coconuts along the shore and then bring them home where dad would take on the task and endure an hour or so of husking and removing the outer skin with a chisel and a hammer. What a labor of love that was! After dad had made the necessary punctures into the coconut with his screwdriver, mother would get out her measuring cup and meticulously measure the coconut milk into four glasses, making sure the amount was exactly the same so we kids wouldn't get in a fight.

Our dad was a Marine and proud of it. We were raised to love the flag, and he made sure we knew and respected what it stood for. He would take us many times out to the base so we could see where he worked as an Air Traffic Controller. We had fun watching the planes take off and land.

Back in 1955, Hawaii wasn't yet a State. I will never forget the day dad put us kids in a little rowboat, took us out into Pearl Harbor so we could see the USS Arizona (the memorial hadn't been built yet) and told us the story about that fateful morning on December 7, 1941. It was an important event in history and dad wanted to make sure we kids knew about it. That day will be forever etched into my memory.

After we returned back to the Mainland, two more children were born—another sister, Mary, and then a little brother, John. So now we were a family of eight!

Like I said, raising six children on a military's salary was, I'm sure, always a challenge for dad. Having access to the Commissary for food and the PX for clothing and other items helped to cut costs, but still I remember times when we didn't have much food on the table. My dad, the man that he was, took on a second job as a custodian at night, cleaning office buildings and then putting on his uniform the next morning and going to work as a Marine. That's what a real man does to feed and support his family.

So now, back in the present, at the end of a year, after Dad had been diagnosed with colon cancer, I knew I wanted to talk to him and tell him what a great dad he was. Mom and dad were living in Sitka, Alaska, and I was living in Southern California, where I had lived my entire life, except for the two years dad was stationed in Hawaii.

To lose someone you love is heartbreaking and tragic at any time, but in some strange kind of way, to know you are dealing with a fatal disease, is a blessing—to know you've been given the gift of having time to say good-bye. There are no words left unsaid.

So I called dad and we had a lovely talk. I told him I knew he wanted to go out and get drunk with his buddies that night instead of meeting my mom. I said, *"You gave up a lot when you married a woman with four small children under the age of seven."* He reassured me he would have done it again, and said he never had any regrets, never.

Just a few short weeks after that call, I was notified dad was failing fast, so I needed to head to Alaska. I will never forget that morning when my sister, Sarah, and I arrived at the airport in Sitka. Our sister, Mary, who lives in Sitka, told us dad was gone. Gone? I wasn't going to get to see dad one last time to tell him how much I loved him? How could this be, and how could God allow this to happen?

I felt like the wind had been knocked out of me. I was numb and I remember collapsing in the bathroom stall. I was angry at

God for taking this wonderful man from our family. He had sacrificed so much for all of us. But because I didn't have Jesus in my life, and I hadn't been to church in years, I had no faith—my faith was zero. In all of this sorrow, I had nothing to hang on to. I didn't know Jesus, or where He was, and because of that, I didn't have the hope of Jesus. I was literally distraught and I just sobbed for days. At the young age of sixty six, our dad's funeral was the day before Father's Day, June 15, 1991, in the National Cemetery in Sitka, Alaska. Sadly, he had passed before he received his Father's Day cards. They were unopened and unread and were buried alongside him that day.

A Surprise Had Been Waiting For Me

It was during this time of my father's passing in Sitka that I went to the beach to collect my thoughts, sob my heart out over the loss of my dad and ask God the question, 'Why'? I was heartbroken and didn't think I would ever pull myself together.

The beauty along the shoreline was absolutely breathtaking. Bald eagles nestled high above in the tall pines keeping their eyes focused below for their next sumptuous meal of salmon, while whales and sea lions passed along in the stillness of Sitka Sound. I stood in awe of the beauty around me and for a moment my mind was being relieved of the anguish I was feeling.

It was on this walk that I looked down and spotted a perfect heart-shaped rock. I picked it up, held it in my hand and thought about what the message of the heart meant to me— love, romance, devotion, cherished, protected, honored, and security. I had never been a collector of anything before, but I knew I wanted to find more of these special rocks. Looking back now, I can see how Jesus was reaching out and wooing me to come to Him for my every need, but I was too blind to see beyond my grief and anguished heart.

A year later, I knew my marriage would be coming to an end; and my father was gone. But life goes on, right? And in some kind of crazy and tumultuous way, it did. My daughter was away at college and my son had graduated from high school. My 24/7 job as a mother, as I knew it, was over. Now that my two kids were raised, I could take a breath.

Unfortunately, I was worried about how my son's life was going, as he had chosen a path that I didn't feel was the right one. He had decided that instead of college, he was going to follow the Grateful Dead! I fretted (mothers are good at that) and was anxious for him.

I will share more about my prodigal son, Aaron, and how God worked in his life a bit later in this story.

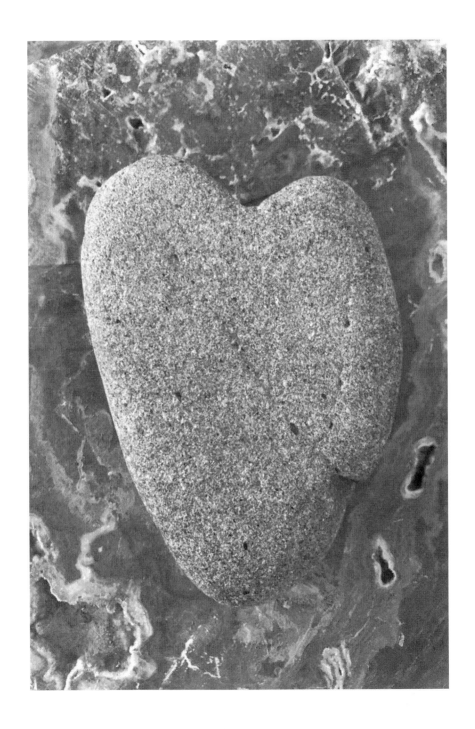

~3~

Sorrow and Suffering

It was good for me to be afflicted
so that I might learn your decrees.
Psalm 119:71

Yet another thread that I will describe to you is somewhat like the previous one, as it includes much pain. But it also marks the beginning of my learning about myself and my discovery of the joy that comes from Christ. As a direct result of losing my job, I met a lovely lady, and through her, I found my way back to the church.

I worked for the Saddleback Valley Unified School District in the city of Mission Viejo, CA, and loved working at the high school where I was around teenagers. I loved all their energy. I looked forward to the pep rallies, marching band, the cheerleaders and going to football games. Then one day I was called into the principal's office.

I was told my job was being eliminated, due to budget cuts, and I would be transferring to the junior high school. I was devastated.

I started sobbing so hard the principal called in another co-worker and asked her to take me for a walk around the track. I just couldn't believe this was happening to me after all I had been going through in my personal life.

One of the secretaries tried to console me and told me about her very best friend, Mary Ann Olsen, a teacher who worked at the school I was being transferred to. I'm sure this secretary gave Mary Ann the heads up and told her about me, and that I would be working there soon. I'm also certain she told her to reach out to me with some TLC. I know Mary Ann was part of God's plan for me as He was guiding me along my shaky path.

At the new school, I did the ordering of supplies for the classrooms and the only contact I actually had with Mary Ann was an occasional pleasantry, or when I placed an order for her.

After a short time, I moved again to another school. After a year there, it was now December, supposedly the happiest holiday of the year, but not for me.

My marriage was over, and one evening I was struggling with the question, 'What am I going to do with my life. Where will I go?' I took a chance and called Mary Ann. I had heard she was single and lived in a large house and would often rent out rooms, so I called her to ask if she might be interested in taking in a boarder. To my surprise she said, *"Sure, come on over and we'll talk."* The date was December 14, 1991.

She gave me the key to her home that night and little did I know that was to be the start of a journey I was about to take.

Like I said, I didn't know Mary Ann very well, but this I did know about her. I knew she was really into Jesus and loved Him deeply. Well, that was fine with me; I was only going to be a boarder. She could do her church thing—just count me out! I was not interested in hearing about her 'loving and faithful God', certainly not after all that I had been through.

I was still reeling from the death of my father, the end of my marriage, my son going down the wrong path, and my unexpected job transfer. I had also undergone a major surgery that had complications. I was running out of steam and had no energy. I had tried so hard to hold it all together, and then realized I could no longer keep the juggling act together.

But God is a master at weaving all things together for good, and He had provided a safe place for me to live while I was going through this sorrowing season of my life. I had a beautiful home to live in, with my own private bath. My clothes that had been carted around from this friend's house to another's house in brown paper 'Lucky' grocery bags (I didn't even own a suitcase) had now found a home in a closet. I also brought along my small collection of heart-rocks that added a sweet touch to my new room. Life was, starting in some small way, to be turning a corner for me.

Mary Ann Was a Real Surprise for Me

Mary Ann was bold and courageous and constantly sharing what she knew about Jesus. I wasn't interested and didn't want to hear it. But she wouldn't give up on me, because as she so often said, *"God will never give up on you. He loves you deeply and He has a plan for you."* She would hold me in her arms as I was sobbing, and she would pray for me.

As Christmas was approaching, which I was dreading, Mary Ann invited me to attend Christmas Eve service with her at her church. I thought to myself, 'What have I got to lose?' I was so sad and depressed and I figured I could cry just as easily in church as I could in my room. So that Christmas Eve was my reintroduction back into church after many, many years of not attending. Unbeknownst to me at the time, I think a tiny seed had been planted in my heart.

I will never forget that Christmas morning, living in someone else's home instead of my own. I came down stairs and saw that Mary Ann was already up having her coffee. She said, *"Merry Christmas! Look, Santa has been here."* I looked towards the fireplace and saw a stocking had been hung for me! It was filled with girly things: lip gloss, hair barrettes, hand lotion, and it was topped off with a fresh orange that had been picked from the back yard. I was moved to tears when I saw it. To think I had only been living with Mary Ann for ten days; yet she had taken the time to make Christmas morning special for me. I was moved by her kindness and compassion for me.

Mary Ann and I were great roommates, although we were opposites in some areas. I do not like wrinkled clothes, ever! I always press whatever I'm wearing, especially for work. So on my first day there I asked Mary Ann if she had an ironing board and where would it be. Her reply was, *"What would it look like?"* Oh no, are you kidding me? She said if she had one it might be in a closet she directed me to. She had lived in her house for many, many years and had tons of items stored in this closet. Sure enough, after digging around and sorting through lots of stuff, I found the ironing board and the iron not far from it.

Living with Mary Ann was quite an adventure. You could say we were kind of like the sitcom back in the seventies, The Odd Couple, starring Jack Klugman and Tony Randall. Remember, Felix, the neat and uptight guy, and then there was Oscar, so laid back and easy going. I told Mary Ann as the weeks went by that we were like the Odd Couple. I'm Felix and you're Oscar. We both laughed our heads off. Yes, we might have been a little mismatched to be roommates, but God knew Mary Ann had a heart of flesh and I had a heart of stone, and for that reason He knew we were a perfect fit. Mary Ann was a joyful messenger of God's love, a love I hadn't experienced yet.

One night I was in the study, ironing my clothes for work the next day. I had on my girly nightgown and was sipping tea. In walks Mary Ann, wearing her flannel plaid two-piece pajamas, sits down at her computer, and pops open a beer. I said, *"Hey,*

Oscar, just look at the two of us." We took it all in and just laughed a good laugh. It was good to be laughing!

Mary Ann was kind of like a religious Erma Bombeck. At first, when the weekend would be approaching, I knew all too well the question that was about to come: *"Donna, are you going to church on Sunday?"* So as not to disappoint my landlady, and to be the perfect tenant, I said, *"Sure, I'm going to church."* She just wouldn't give up!

After I had moved in, she told me that my sleep might be interrupted on Thursday mornings because she had a women's Bible Study that met at 6:00 AM. Well, I couldn't fathom giving up sleep to meet with a bunch of women. ,Besides, who wanted to sit around, read the Bible, and pray? That was not the lifestyle for me, and it was not going to be a part of my plan for my life! I didn't want to hang out with a bunch of church people . . . after all—they're so boring, and they're certainly no fun.

At the bottom of the staircase, Mary Ann had a humongous Bible that was always opened, and sitting on top of some kind of pedestal that I had to pass every time I went up to my bedroom. As I walked past this Bible, I would put my hand up to shield my eyes, so as not look at the pages. I would say, *"No thank you, Jesus. I am not interested today or ever!"*

One day Mary Ann gave me a book to read called **Hind's Feet on High Places**. I didn't want to read her book, but in order to shut her up I said, 'Ok, I will read it.' The title comes from the Bible verse from the book of Habakkuk.

The Lord God is my strength
and He will make my feet like Hind's feet,
and He will make me walk upon my high places.
Habakkuk 3:19.

Like I said, this woman would not give up. And so, through my tears and desperation, I relented and read the book. It was about a girl named **Much-Afraid**, who sets out on her spiritual journey through difficult places with the Shepherd and her two companions, Sorrow and Suffering. Her life is transformed by her union with God when she reaches new heights of love, joy and victory.

Oh, and by the way, this girl, **Much-Afraid**, had tied around her waist a belt that held a leather pouch to collect the rocks she had found along her path. I said, *"Mary Ann, Much-Afraid collects rocks too!"* She replied, *"Yes, I know. Keep reading."* As **Much-Afraid** began to trust in the Shepherd and learn new lessons, she would build an altar and each time, there would be a special rock nearby. She would pick it up, thank her Lord and put it in her pouch.

I Began to Learn

As she journeyed along her spiritual path, God planted the seed of Love in her heart. And as she grew in faith, **Much-Afraid** was given a new name, Grace and Glory. Her companions were no longer Suffering and Sorrow, but were turned into Joy and Peace.

I was beginning to realize the only way to reach the 'high places' of victory and union with God was by learning to accept day by day the conditions and tests permitted by God and by repeated laying down of our own will and acceptance of His.

When I finished the last page, I broke down and cried. I identified so closely with the character in the book. You see, that story was about me. I realized that I was just like **Much-Afraid**. My life was consumed with Suffering and Sorrow.

46

I had anxiety, worry, low self-esteem and tremendous fears. I was afraid of heights, terrified to get on an airplane or ride in an elevator. All of these things kept me immobilized and shut off from life itself.

It was so hard and difficult to put on a happy face and go to work each day, where no one had a clue as to what I was going through. I would get up ten minutes earlier each morning to allow time to put cold Lipton ice tea bags over my eyelids to take the swelling out. My eyelids were a mess from all the tears I was purging. (Let me tell you, that trick really works, and I should have bought stock in Lipton from the amount of tea bags I was going through.) So off to work I'd go, and when the day was finished, as I was walking towards my car, the tears would be brimming over my eyelids. Then they came in full force once I was safe inside my car. I was going through the refiner's fire!

I don't remember the exact day, but gradually something started to happen within me and my soul was awakened. A tiny seed had been planted in my heart. Maybe it was hearing those beautiful hymns I remembered as a child and being around others who said they were praying for me.

I'm not sure, but it was like the bones of my soul had been dried up and dead for many, many years and now, slowly, my soul was coming back to life and I was feeling my emotions in a very different and new way. I discovered I had this insatiable appetite to be connected to church and to hear God's word.

This realization hit me when Mary Ann took a trip to Spain for two weeks and, guess where I was on Sunday mornings? I was in church!

I didn't have to be there because Mary Ann was in Spain on the other side of the world. She'd never know if I were in church or not. But, I'd know. I needed church and I needed God in my life.

A small mound of heart-rocks was now growing in the corner of my bedroom, rocks that would be taking on a new meaning for me soon. It's not that I went out searching for these stones to start a collection, as I had never collected anything, but looking back I know it was God who was placing them in my path. At the time, I had no idea what I would do with them. I just loved the beauty of them, as they were all different sizes and colors.

At that time I had finished reading the book, **Hind's Feet on High Places,** and I had been impressed by the character, *Much-Afraid*, who picked up rocks and would build an alter and give thanks to God for the lessons she was learning as she trusted in Him.

I was still in a very fragile state, and I was acting like the character *Much-Afraid*. I was on my spiritual journey and, looking back, that little pile of heart-rocks was my altar to God—my reminder of His love for me.

As I started reading the Bible I came to believe that Jesus was, and is, my rock, my strength and my refuge. Friends would comment on my heart-rocks and I would start to give them away one by one, and God would always replenish the pile.

~4~

Born Again

Therefore, if anyone is in Christ,
he is a new creation;
the old has gone, the new has come.
2 Corinthians 5:17

My life to this point had been one of many ups and downs, as you have seen. My spiritual journey had a similar pattern, some of which I have already related. Here is a little fuller explanation of how that evolved. In my new-found interest in going to church and allowing myself to consider a place for God in my life, I began to wonder, '*What is a born again Christian? What does that phrase actually mean?*' To me, it defined hypocrites and 'holy rollers'. No thanks! That's not the life for me or anything I'd ever believe in or be interested in.

But then I started to read the Bible, God's love letter to us. What a fabulous book! I didn't remember it being so full of so much valuable information when I was younger. Mary Ann would say, *"The Bible is your Owner's Manual for how to live a good and happy life."* How right she was. Just as we receive an Owner's Manual whenever we purchase a new car, or an appliance, to help us know how to care for it, the Bible guides us in how to live a happy and joyful life. It's full of wisdom straight from God, so whatever question we might have, we will always find the answer in the Bible.

Like Nicodemus, I, too, wondered how a person could be born again when you've already been born once. But Jesus sure set the record straight when He said,

51

I tell you the truth;
no one can see the kingdom of God
unless he is born again.
Flesh gives birth to flesh,
but the Spirit gives birth to spirit.
You should not be surprised at my saying,
"You must be born again.
John 3:3, 7

I have three sisters: Sarah, Jacqueline and Mary. Jacqueline and Mary became Christians way before I ever saw the light. I remember making fun of them, mocking them, saying things like, "You don't really believe all that stuff, do you?" These comments were mostly directed at my sister Jacqueline, because Mary lived so far away in Alaska.

Jacqueline would patiently listen to my comments and she always kept her composure. She would state what she believed and what she knew the facts to be, but always with grace in her voice.

Sometime in February of 1993, in God's perfect timing, Jesus touched my hardened heart of stone. He knew I needed something I didn't have. So at the age of forty-four, I received Jesus into my heart as my Lord and Savior and I became 'born-again'. I was a new creation in Christ and once I had tasted this new life, I knew I would never be content with the old. And like ***Much Afraid***, God turned my brokenness into wholeness and put joy and peace back into my life.

Through God's spirit He gave me a new heart.

"I will give you a new heart and put a new spirit within you; I will take the heart of stone out of your flesh and give you a heart of flesh.
Ezekiel 36:26

I had a new heart. I learned to listen to God's voice, to follow Him, and to trust in His plan for me.

As I grew closer to God and started to develop a relationship with Him, all the hurts, sorrow, bitterness and anger slowly started to lift from my heart. I learned the power of forgiveness. I had held onto so much hurt for so many years that I had developed a hardened, callused heart. I had no room for joy in my heart. I questioned where was this loving, protecting Jesus when bad, evil things were happening to me? Jesus was right there beside me, weeping with me and feeling my pain. I had doubted God's love for me. I was angry at God. I know now, Jesus never abandoned me—I had abandoned Him. Jesus knocked patiently at the door of my heart until I was ready to invite Him in.

And so, I gradually started to move out of my isolated world that was once full of fears, worries and sadness and began to enjoy this beautiful life God had given me. I'm doing things today I could never have done twenty-five years ago.

I have apologized to both Jacqueline and Mary for the way I behaved with them before finding Jesus for myself, and I have thanked them for loving me unconditionally. So now, fast forward, and here I am, a 'born again' Christian, and I wanted Sarah to know the same joy I had, and the promise of eternal life, so I started praying for her, along with prayers for my daughter and my son.

I invited Sarah many times to come to a Women's Retreat with me, but she always declined. Then one year she said she'd think about it. She called a few days later, and said yes, she would go! That was in April of 2001 and she accepted Christ at that retreat. She called me the next day, thanking me for inviting her, even when she had said no in the past, and then she said, *"Thank you for never giving up on me."* I told her I would never give up on her, and I knew God wouldn't either.

Today, I can ride in an airplane anxiety fee and enjoy the beauty below me. Yes, I actually look out the window! I can ride an elevator! No longer do I have to trudge up flights of stairs to visit my doctor. Taking the stairs is healthier, but now if I'm pressed for time, I have a choice. All these fears have been erased from my life because I know I have a Shepherd who is with me every minute of every day. We have the best security system available to us, our beloved Shepherd who says,

> I am with you always, to the very end of the age.
> *Matthew 28:20*

Oh, and here's a little side note . . . guess what? I love to go to church! I love to sit around with a bunch of women and read the Bible and pray. I love to hang out with church people who, by the way, are lots of fun and not boring at all! And that's because we are filled with the joy of the Lord and walk in His light.

Just as God wooed Moses with the burning bush, God, in His clever way used a heart-shaped rock to open the 'eyes' of my heart. For He knew I was seeing the world through 'earthly eyes', not the eyes that were set on Jesus.

Through God's amazing grace, He opened my heart and, like **Much-Afraid**, planted His seed of Love. I was no longer a lost, long-legged, shabby sheep, bleating and wandering aimlessly without a Shepherd. When I kept Jesus as my focal point, all the pieces fell into place and I saw the world around me from His perspective. I knew it was to be the beginning of a lifelong love story for me!

I'm a born again Christian and proud of it. I am not ashamed of the gospel and to say I follow Jesus Christ. Why would I be? I've been given the greatest gift in my life! I have tasted and know that the Lord is, indeed, very good! I have never been happier in my entire life than I am today. I glorify and praise Jesus for the abundant blessings He has given me. My tears today are tears of joy and thanksgiving. I know I don't have to be perfect anymore. Jesus loves me just the way I am.

To accept Jesus as your Lord and Savior is the most important decision you will ever make for your eternal future, and statistics are pretty right on . . . ten out of ten people are going to die. I know I am a sinner, but I've been saved by grace. I've been given a gift I could never pay for or earn. It's God's gift to me through His unmerited favor. I have the assurance that when my mansion is completed, and the Lord calls me home, I will be ushered into Heaven. I stand in awe of this glorious promise!

~5~

Rock Stories

As I explained on the first page, all of this is really about two separate stories, each of which overlays and is entwined with the other. One story is about the twists and turns of my life. The other is about my passion for heart-rocks and for sharing them with people. Let's turn to several stories about them right now.

I'm remembering the day I retired from the Saddleback Valley School District. Everyone I worked with knew of my faith and how much I loved Jesus. But there were others in the different departments of the district office that I didn't know well, or where they were on their own faith journey, or if they even had a faith. But most of them, especially my close co-workers, knew of my heart-rocks and the story behind them.

To bid farewell on my last day I decided to bring a basketful of rocks and pass them out to everyone. So as I went from department to department and passed out a heart-rock, I would say to the person, *"May this be a reminder that God loves you and He will always be your Rock and Refuge!"* Everyone was thrilled at this little gift.

When someone retired from the school district, it was pretty common knowledge that you would see that retired person again soon, because they come back as subs for different positions. It wasn't long before I was in that category.

When I would sub, I remember having to deliver or pick up something at the district office. As I passed the different departments, people would call out to me, *"Hey Donna, I see you're back. Thank you for my heart-rock, it's still on my desk and I know God loves me!"* Many others had similar comments. It gave me such joy to know that after so long, whenever I was working as a sub, people still had their rock proudly displayed on their desk.

My husband and I lived in a gated community in Mission Viejo, and we had a landscaping company that worked each day keeping the trees and shrubs in tiptop shape. When you see these people on a regular basis, you come to know them. It was always fun to pass out a heart-rock to some of the gardeners, even if they really didn't understand what I was trying to tell them. The shape of the heart is pretty self-explanatory, and I would point up to the heavens, and I think they got it.

One day as I was leaving to go on my walk around the lake, the supervisor for the gardeners came driving down my street. He would usually wave or honk his horn, but this time he actually stopped his van and rolled down the window. He said, *"I have my rock right here (he pointed to the dashboard) so I can see it always. I'm a recovering alcoholic, and this rock is my reminder that I can do this. I CAN stay sober, with God as my rock that I can stand upon. I know He is always with me, each step of the way."*

Well, I had no idea he was a recovering alcoholic. It gave me such joy that he felt safe in sharing that with me. He wanted to thank me for giving him that tangible reminder of God's love and presence.

I love coffee and I was a regular at our local donut shop.(Not for the donuts, but for the coffee!) I loved chatting with the owners, who were from Cambodia, sharing my faith with them. We were very good friends for several years.

One day a young man came in to get some donuts, and for whatever reason, he started talking with me. He told me he was out of work and was recovering from drug addiction. He seemed so lost and sad. I tried to encourage him, and I told him I would be praying for him. Then I remembered I had a special heart-rock in the trunk of my car that I was planning to give to someone else. But at that moment I knew God wanted me to give it to this young man. I told him I had something I wanted to give him and ran out to my car.

I gave him the heart-rock and shared what it represented. I told him I would pray that God would lead and guide him to employment and to keep him clean and sober. I said, *"Remember, God always allows U-turns."* He became so overwhelmed with emotion, I became teary-eyed, too.

When I attended my first conference on Care and Kindness at the Crystal Cathedral, I remember passing out a heart-rock to each person who sat at my table. It was such a great ice breaker and a fun way to open up conversations, especially if you're talking about our ever-loving God.

There was a gentleman from North Carolina, such a godly, spiritual man, who attended every year, as I did. When he and his wife decided to vacation in Southern California, my husband and I met them down at the beach for dinner. The four of us had such a great time, and we kept in touch through the years, exchanging Christmas cards and emails periodically.

Two years ago I received an email from him letting me know his email address had changed. I wrote back to thank him and wanted to know how things were going for him and his wife. To my surprise, he called and said, *"Donna, are you still collecting those heart-rocks? The one you gave me so many years ago, I carried it in my pocket every day and somehow I must have pulled it out with my keys and I lost it. If you could spare to give me another one, I would be so ever grateful."* Of course I told him, 'No problem'—I would get one in the mail to him soon. I sent him two, one for him and one to pass on to someone else. I heard back from him and he was so thrilled that I had sent him not one, but two heart-rocks!

I was a Deacon for the home-bounds at my church in Mission Viejo and loved to minister to those special people who were unable to attend church. I would read the Bible to them and pray, and we would just talk about God and His goodness. It was through one of these members at my church that I came to know and admire her sister, who was on hospice and dying of cancer.

Although I hadn't met this woman, when I learned of her illness, I knew I wanted her to have a heart-rock. In just a matter of days I received a note that touched my heart and gave me a glimpse of her deep faith in God.

She thanked me for the heart-rock and said, *"And now I have been blessed by it. The Lord surely is my Rock. I feel His presence constantly. I know He is always with me, and so I have that marvelous peace that passes all understanding."* She closed by saying, *"I am looking forward to the time when I will dwell in His house forever."*

I knew I had to meet this special lady in person and set a time for a visit. As I was driving to her house, it dawned on me I would be visiting someone who was dying of a terminal illness. I became nervous, not knowing how I would reach out to her. What could I say that would comfort her, and how would I pray?

She was weak, but had a cheerful attitude that put any nervousness or fears I had to rest. We talked about our husbands, children, and grandchildren, and then we talked about her illness, death and what heaven would be like.

I will never forget what she said to me next. With her arms crossed upon her chest she said, *"I am really looking forward to this, Donna. I think it is going to be marvelous, I truly do. And my Howard (her husband who had predeceased her) is waiting for me and I miss him so. Of course, I will miss my family and friends here, but they'll be along someday."*

Wow! What faith she had. I had not ministered to <u>her</u> that day, but rather, she had ministered to <u>me</u>. She was living proof of God's word, right before my eyes. It was apparent she was growing weaker each day, but her faith and love for God was growing deeper and stronger. She possessed a spirit of faith I knew I wanted.

When my husband's job took us to Colorado in 2007, we were excited for the adventure. We had a lovely home with a huge basement and a lake out back. The sunrises were spectacular— each and every morning was a glorious sight to see.

Because our neighborhood was a new development, we, along with several of our neighbors, were not expecting the garage floors to be sinking and the driveways to be cracking and shifting. This was the result of the builders not using re-bar when they poured the driveways and garage floors.

One of our neighbors discovered a great company who would tear up the old concrete and pour the new garage floors and driveways, so we got on the list to have ours repaired.

When the owner of the company (his name was Bill Cushman) came to inspect our garage floor and what would be entailed in the job, he saw all of my heart-rocks that were in several wire baskets stacked up in the garage. He commented on them and asked why I had so many, and what was I going to do with them. I love a captive audience, so of course I started to share my story with him. He thought they were great, and then continued on with his inspection of the driveway.

Before he left, he told me his wife was having some medical issues and asked if he could have one to give her. He said maybe it would bring her some hope and comfort, as she was in a lot of pain. Of course I let him pick out the one he thought she would like, and I wrote Psalm 18:2 on it.

> The Lord is my rock,
> my fortress and my deliverer,
> My God is my rock in whom I take refuge.
> He is my shield, and the horn of my salvation,
> my stronghold.

Before he left, he mentioned that his son, who was in high school, was facing finals the next week and he was all stressed out about it. He asked if he could pick out a heart-rock for him as well. I said, *"Of course, help yourself."* Then he mentioned his daughter, and I said, *"How many kids do you have? Take as many as you need."* He was overjoyed.

Bill and his crew were people I was seeing just about every day, since they were replacing many garage floors and driveways on our street. They became like an extended family to us and all the neighbors.

When it came time for our driveway to be poured, Bill said to me, *"Donna, How would you like it if we were to put one of your heart-rocks in the driveway after we pour the concrete."* Are you kidding me? I said, *"I would love it! Would you really do that, could you?"* He responded and said, *"Of course we can do that, and I will even stamp the scripture Psalm 18:2 in the center of the driveway."* Well, as much as I would have loved that addition too, I didn't think the Homeowners

Association would go for it, so we just had the heart-rock placed down near the sidewalk where anyone walking by would see it. I sure do miss that driveway that has the mark of God's love in it!

Living in Colorado gave me the opportunity to grow my harvest of heart-rocks, as they are virtually everywhere in that state. Many people would contact me and ask if I would send a heart-rock to a family member or a dear friend who was going through a tough time. Of course, I knew God was putting all those rocks in my path for a purpose—to bless others of His love for them.

I was a regular at our local post office, mailing a heart-rock off to another state, and sometimes overseas to Europe. The clerk at the counter would ask the usual question about whether there was anything flammable, liquid or dangerous in my package. So I would be blessed to tell them about my heart-rocks. One gentleman always had a beautiful picture of a cross sitting on his counter. I commented on it and said, *"I can see you love Jesus too."* He said, *"I couldn't get through life without Him."* That was always a treat to go to his window to mail my heart-rocks, and I told him I would have a heart-rock for him the next time I came in. I gave him a very beautiful rock I found in Alaska. It sat perfectly on his desk for all to see, but he would put it away at the end of his shift because he didn't want it taken.

Through my many trips to the post office, this man eventually told me his co-worker, who didn't believe in Jesus, needed to have a heart-rock. So I took advantage of that and started to go to his co-worker's window to mail my rocks away. It opened a dialogue when he asked the question about anything being flammable, liquid or dangerous, and I told him he would be getting a heart-rock, too. Just a reminder that God loved him. He had a little bit of a smirk on his face, but underneath I think he was pleased by what I had to say, and on my next trip in he, too, had the gift of a rock. I told him he could use it as a paper weight, as they are very functional and can be used for many things.

My husband and I made several trips a year back to Southern California to visit family and friends. Five days before we were to leave on one of our trips out, my husband's nephrologist called and said something showed up on one of his tests. He said he needed to get an MRI done to find out what was going on with his kidneys. Because we were set to leave in just a few days, the doctor pushed to have the test done immediately. The MRI showed Bill had a mass on his left kidney.

Since Bill had had surgery for prostate cancer in 2003 at City of Hope in California, we called to see if Bill could be seen there. We were given the results to share with the doctor and he confirmed Bill did in fact have a mass; there was a 90% chance of it being cancer. We scheduled the date for the surgery, went on to visit with family and friends, and then returned back to Colorado to get things done in preparation for the surgery.

It was on our drive back to Colorado that we were blessed when we stopped for lunch at a Cracker Barrel in Gallup, New Mexico. Our food server was a young man who was very personable. He asked where we were coming from and where did we live. We told him we would be passing through again in a few weeks and told him about Bill's upcoming surgery. I gave him a heart-rock (I always seem to have them with me) and he was so happy to get it. He told us he was a Christian and loved Jesus.

When he brought us our food he said, *"Guess what? One of our Deacons is here for dinner on the other side and I would love to bring her over so the both of us can pray over your husband, if that would be ok with you."*

"Ok? Of course, go and get her!" I said. The food server introduced us to the Deacon and they both placed hands upon my husband, and she said the most beautiful prayer, right there in Cracker Barrel.

On our drive out for the surgery, we stopped at that Cracker Barrel again, hoping to see this young man who had blessed us that day, but he no longer worked there. I even called the church where he said he attended, but no one ever answered the phone and there was no voice message I could leave. We never saw him again and I often wonder if he was an angel God had placed in our path that day.

There was another great restaurant that we found on our drives out to California. I had read about this person in my Guidepost magazine and was fascinated by his story. His name is Tim Harris and he was the owner of Tim's Place, the country's only restaurant owner with Down Syndrome. Tim's Place was located in Albuquerque, New Mexico, and I knew I wanted to meet this kid in person. And . . . I knew I wanted to give him a heart-rock.

The article said that Tim greeted every customer who walked through the door, and he greeted them with a hug. He even had a hug-o-meter on the wall that kept a record of every hug he gave. I couldn't wait to meet him and give him a heart-rock.

When we arrived, Tim was right there to greet us at the door with a hug. I told him I was a hugger, too, and that my license plate was 'GVAHUG'. He was just a delight to talk with and hear all about his restaurant, which had been his dream ever since he was a little boy. He took us on a tour and showed us the medals he had won in the Special Olympics, something that is close to my husband's heart. I told him I had brought something special to give him and showed him the rock. I told him the story and what it represented. He was so happy, jumping up and down and dancing. He wanted to video me giving him the rock so he could put it on Facebook. We told him we would be back again on our next trip out.

On that next trip out we received our hug from Tim, and he remembered us and mentioned the heart-rock, but this time it was a sad day for him. He told us his best friend that he played basketball with had unexpectedly passed away just a couple of days ago. Then he started to cry. He apologized and said he had to get it together because he was at work and he had a job to do. My heart was breaking for him and I told him his tears were precious to the Lord and they showed the depth of his love for his friend.

And tears are healing. They were a part of God's blueprint when He designed us. Our tear ducts are important for our healing. I reminded him of the heart-rock and that God would be his strength and refuge during this time of sadness and sorrow. We all hugged and he said he had his heart-rock in a special place.

We never saw Tim again and learned a few years ago that he closed the restaurant and moved to Denver to be near his girlfriend. We were sad to hear he was moving to Denver, as we had now moved back to California. When he closed his restaurant after five years, the hug-o-meter read 75,402 hugs!

At Christmas, my sister and I were shopping at Nordstrom. While my sister was making a purchase in the men's department, I was browsing around and came upon a display case that was filled with men's sunglasses. The thing that caught my eye was that the glasses were sitting on top of a bunch of rocks.

I thought to myself, wouldn't it be something if there was a heart-rock in there? So I started to scan the case and, lo and behold! I spotted two heart-rocks! I ran over to the clerk, who was helping my sister, and said, *"Excuse me, but the case over there, the one with the rocks in it,"* and I started telling him about my rock collection and asked if I could have the two in the case.

He said, *"Lady, we found those rocks out in the gutter."* I said, *"I don't care where you found them, God made them and I'd like to have them."*

He rolled his eyes and followed me back to the display case. When I pointed out the rocks, he gasped and said, *"Hey, you're right, they are shaped like hearts."* I smiled and said, *"I know, they're heart-rocks. Now, may I have them?"* He got out his key, unlocked the case and gave me the rocks.

That was the best purchase I brought home that day, and it didn't cost me a penny!

~6~

Blessed Beyond Measure

You have captured my heart. . . .
Song of Solomon 4:9

I've been telling you about two great loves in my life — my love for Jesus Christ, and my love for heart-rocks. Those two loves blessed me richly. But now, another love was about to be added. Follow along with me as I tell my crazy love story of meeting Bill.

I've been married to Bill (William) Bond Sprague for over twenty-five years. Many people often ask us how we met, or where we met. We are more than happy to share how our love story unfolded—how it all began.

We both used the same divorce attorney, William (Bill) S. Hulsy, and he was our 'matchmaker', the one who put us together. He was even the Best Man at our wedding!

Bill, my attorney, had called me at work one day and invited me to attend his Office Christmas party. He said he had someone he wanted me to meet, someone who was a very nice man. Those were his words! I told him upfront that I was not interested in meeting any man—I wasn't ready for that. I wasn't looking for anyone, and I was enjoying my single life; I was feeling quite happy where I was. I was quite content with my connection to a church, and a Women's Bible study.

He said he was going to mail me an invitation anyway, in case I changed my mind.

Christmas was coming soon and I was remembering the last one. I was remembering where I had been emotionally that previous year, and all the turmoil, and what I had gone through . . . dreading the holidays. But I had grown a lot in the past year and, most of all, it was that my spiritual life was growing. I was now a Christian and learning more about Jesus and why He came to earth to save us. God opened the 'eyes' of my heart, and I was seeing Christmas in a different way, a deeper way of what the true meaning of Christmas really was. I was now, for the first time in my life, looking forward to this holy holiday and preparing my heart with deep devotion and gratitude for the birth of my Savior, Jesus Christ. I loved looking at my heart-rocks and marveled at how my collection of these special stones continued to grow; the new meaning that they represented was beginning to grow in my own heart. It was Christmas, I loved Jesus and I was joyful!

The invitation for the Christmas party that my attorney had said he would send soon arrived. Since I love people and I especially love parties, I decided I would attend after all. However, I was not interested in meeting any man! I would go, enjoy the festivities, the good food I was certain would be there, and share in the season of Christmas. The date of the party was December 17, 1992.

I had a grand time that evening, chatting and meeting some wonderful people, many who had gone through a divorce like I had. It was interesting to hear their stories about how they were rebuilding their lives. Many of them, like me, had been on a road that had many twists and turns, and some hard switchbacks.

In return, I shared with them the exciting trip I had taken earlier in the year to Ireland. As I was driving one day, and listening to a radio station, there was an announcement that the station would be going to Dublin, Ireland, to march in the St.

Patrick's Day parade. They were going to take as many listeners as wanted to go. I thought to myself, 'Wow, wouldn't that be something . . . to go to Ireland and celebrate my birthday the day before marching in a parade there?' (Remember, my birthday is March 16th, *John 3:16*.) And because I was no longer afraid to get on an airplane, I decided I would go for it. I contacted the station, signed up, and looked forward to celebrating my birthday in Ireland!

Three months after the Christmas party, I received a phone call. Mary Ann answered the phone and said it was for me; a man was on the line, but she didn't recognize who it could be. I took the phone and said, *"Hello"*. The voice on the other end said, *"Happy Birthday, Donna. This is Bill Sprague."* I said, *"Who?"*, and he replied, *"Bill Sprague. I met you at Hulsy's Christmas party."* Well, I did not remember meeting any guy named Bill Sprague that night.

I said, *"Well, I have two questions for you. How did you know today was my birthday and how did you get my phone number?"* He reminded me how I shared about my trip to Ireland to celebrate my birthday and march in the parade. Being an engineer, he must have marked his calendar for March 16th. He said he called the attorney's office and they gave him my number. Well, I was furious over that!

Then Bill asked if I'd like to go out to dinner the very next night. What? Did this guy really think I didn't have a life that he could call me on a Friday night and I'd be available the next night? I told him, *"No, thank you. I already had plans."* I really didn't, but that's what I told him. We said our good-byes and hung up. Then I called attorney Bill!

He got right on the phone, and I let him have it. How dare you give out my number to this Bill Sprague, who just called me and asked me out! He said he didn't give out my number; it must have been his secretary. Then he said, *"But if I were you,*

I'd go out with Bill Sprague. He's a wonderful man, and you're a wonderful lady, and I think you would have a lot in common." Since he had handled Bill's divorce, too, he knew both of our backgrounds.

I calmed down and figured I would <u>not</u> be hearing again from this Bill Sprague; and, by the way, I had absolutely no recollection of who he was.

Bill was indeed persistent

About two weeks later he called again and asked me out for the following week. So for some strange reason, I said yes. It was an afternoon date. He took me to play miniature golf and then to Island's Restaurant, where we had a hamburger, and I was home before the sun went down. Yes, Bill was kind and polite, but there was no connection or attraction at all, and I supposed he was probably feeling the same way. I figured I had seen the last of him.

About this time, I had purchased a condo and I was excited about moving into my own little nest. I was busy packing and doing all the things that go along with a move when Bill called again, asking for a date. I used my moving as an excuse to turn him down, thinking he would take the hint, but instead he offered to help me move. I did <u>not</u> want to feel obligated to this man, so I thanked him politely for his offer and told him I had family and friends that would be helping me. I also let him know that I would be very busy for the next couple of weeks and to please not call.

Well, guess what? Two weeks later to the day, he called again.

I figured why not go out again. What would be the harm? He's a nice and polite man and so we had a few more dates going out to dinner, to the movies, or walks on the beach. Of course, I shared with him my heart-rocks and how God had used one to draw His lost sheep back into the fold. By this time we have had a total of four dates with no kiss, no hand holding, no arm around the waist—nothing. I am still not attracted to this guy.

A few days before Memorial Day, Bill called and wanted to get together for a barbeque on that Monday. I told him I didn't relish driving on the freeways on a holiday (Bill was living in Cypress, about a 45 minute drive from me) and suggested we make it another time. But he already had it all planned out. He would bring the fixings for the barbeque to my house. And he sure did. Steaks, bread, wine, the whole nine yards. So as long as I didn't have to drive the freeways, I said, *"Yes"*.

I will never forget when the meal was prepared and we sat down to dinner, Bill asked if I would mind if he said Grace. I had never been with a man who wanted to pray before a meal, and I was really struck by his request. Bill was an official for USA Track and Field, and he had officiated for the Special Olympics the day before. As he started to pray, he thanked God for all the people who participated in the Special Olympics. And then he began to cry. I thought to myself— this man truly has a tender and compassionate heart.

The meal was delicious and we had a great evening. But soon it was time for him to leave, as we both had to go to work in the morning. I thanked him for making the drive, bringing all the food and preparing it. I thanked him especially for the prayer he had said, telling him how special it was. Without saying a word, Bill took my face in his hands, drew me to him and kissed me. And I knew at that moment that there was something definitely there! A kiss can really go deep down into your soul. I had butterflies and I felt like I was in high school again.

On his drive home, Bill called to tell me a song had just come on the radio and it made him think of me. I asked him what the song was and he said, **The Platters, "I've Only Got Eyes for You."** Ok, so now I am thinking . . . there is really something special about this Bill Sprague. It was May 31, 1993, and after that Memorial Day evening, we saw each other on a regular basis.

About a month later, Bill said, *"You know, I think I'm falling in love with you."* Well I certainly didn't want to hear that! Yes, he was a great guy, but I wasn't ready for that kind of relationship, especially if it could lead to marriage. So I tried talking him out of it, telling him he was just infatuated with me, that holding a woman in your arms feels nice, but it doesn't mean you're falling in love. He didn't argue with me, but said, matter-of-factly, *"Ok, I won't argue with you, but I believe if it's in God's plan that we be together, He will make it happen."* I thought to myself, this is a very patient man, and I totally accepted his comment. We continued with the dating.

Bill called towards the end of June and asked if he could escort me to my church. I thought that was a lovely gesture, and said it would be fine. Sunday morning, when he arrived, he told me to close my eyes . . . that he had something for me. I'm thinking to myself — it better not be a ring, because I am not accepting it! I closed my eyes and Bill said, *"I know you want this relationship to go slow, so now we're back in high school and I'm asking you if you'll go steady with me."* Then he placed a gold chain over my head that held a CIF football charm from his high school, Long Beach Poly. Again, I was touched by his sweetness, and said, *"Yes. I would love to go steady with you!"*

Next would be the Senior Prom. Remember, money was tight when I was growing up and I never had the opportunity to attend a prom. Since I was working at the high school, I was asked if I would like to chaperone the prom; I would be allowed to bring a date if I wanted. So I mentioned it to Bill and he said he would love to take me to the Prom! On the day of the dance, a beautiful wrist corsage was delivered to my office. (Bill sure had this courting thing down to a science.) I loved him dearly for all the ways he made me feel so special, and like I was back in high school!

I wore that gold chain with the CIF football every single day until Bill proposed to me on November 11, 1993. With that proposal, he used a darling ring he had bought that had a red heart in the center and small rhinestones on each side. It cost $20! I treasured that ring and always will. But on our tenth wedding anniversary, Bill surprised me with a replica of that little ring. But this one was real gold and had a heart-shaped ruby with diamonds on each side. Still, that $20 rhinestone ring will always be priceless to me.

We set our wedding date for February 19, 1994, at 9:00 AM on a Saturday morning. The night before, we had a small rehearsal dinner at a restaurant across the street from our church. As the evening got underway, a huge electrical storm hit with torrential rain, thunder and lightning.

We were in a panic thinking about our wedding the next morning, and the reception that would be taking place, partly outdoors. When the rehearsal dinner was over, we went over to the church, stood beneath the cross with our umbrella, hoping we wouldn't get struck by lightning, and thanked God for bringing us together, for the love we shared for one another, and asking for His blessings to be upon our wedding in the morning and to calm the storm.

When I woke up on my wedding day, the sun was indeed shining, and the skies were clear as a bell. God had heard our prayer from the night before. As our ceremony got underway, our pastor started out by saying, *"God seems to be smiling in a sparkly way this morning. The sun has broken loose, almost as if the heavens decided to celebrate a little bit with Bill and Donna."*

That glorious morning, the Lord, in His amazing love, took us up in His arms and blessed us. We declared our love for one another and we became 'one'.

I am my beloved's and my beloved is mine.
I had found the one whom my soul loves.
Song of Solomon 3:4

William Hulsy, our matchmaker and Best Man at our wedding, gave the toast which was a poem he had written just for us.

To Donna and Bill

I once had two sad clients who were feeling a might bad,
So to my Christmas party they came in order to feel glad,
To introduce the two of them, I thought I'd take a chance,
Not thinking that the meeting would turn into true romance.

They met, they laughed, they drank, they talked,
To home they would not go,
So in a country bar we walked,
And to my lawyer's bag of tricks, I added cupids bow.

Why should it be that only dogs,
Are entitled to one bite?
To try again in life for love,
Is also humans' right.

You know how the story goes,
The rest is destiny,
How love blooms and blossoms,
Is such a mystery.

They had so much in common,
That it didn't take much time,

78

Before they said their wedding vows,
Within the octave of St. Valentine.

I give you Bill and Donna.
To them we wish the best,
To have and hold each other,
Through years of happiness.

So pop the cork and fill the glass,
And someone tap the keg,
Let's toast our hosts and wish the best,
To Bill and Donna Sprague.

William S. Hulsy

~7~

The Armor of God

Blessed is the nation Whose God is the Lord.
Psalm 33:12

It was so exciting to see how widely my interest in these heart-rocks was spreading; to see what a variety of situations they led me into; and the wonderful responses I got about them, everywhere I went. Never would I have thought that they would lead to a fantastic connection to people in the military!

In 2007, my husband's job transferred us to Denver, Colorado, which was quite a change. Bill and I were both born and raised in Southern California. I had never lived in a place where there were actual changes of the seasons, and I had never seen snow fall out of the sky before. I was a beach girl who still loves to wear flip-flops. Living in Colorado was going to be different for sure, but Bill said it would be a fun adventure. And an adventure it was.

Before our move, we prayed for God to help us find the right home, and to bless us with a loving church family where we could grow in our faith. We prayed about our new community, wherever that would be.

God is good and He is faithful. We found the perfect house in a great neighborhood, and the sweetest little church, First Presbyterian Church of Littleton.

God had the perfect plan when He took us to Colorado. There were heart-rocks everywhere, and I was in heaven! It wasn't long before my collection started growing by leaps and bounds and I knew it would be put to good use as I shared God's love with all the new neighbors and friends I would be meeting.

Martha Cercy was our next door neighbor. The very first snow we had was so exciting for me because this would be the first time I actually saw snowflakes falling from the sky. I ran outside with my flip-flops on, looked up to the heavens and started singing a verse from Julie Andrews, 'My Favorite Things'.

> *"Girls in white dresses with blue satin sashes;*
> *Snowflakes that stay on my nose and eyelashes;*
> *Silver-white winters that melt into springs'*
> *These are a few of my favorite things…"*

Well, I am not a singer, that's for sure, but the Lord says to make a joyful noise unto Him, and I did that day—with nearly frozen toes!

As the snow began to melt a few days later, I was taking in the beauty of it all, and glanced over at Martha's deck, where I spotted a message from God. On the back of one of her patio chairs, the snow had melted into the shape of a heart! I grabbed my camera to take a photo of it, but couldn't quite capture the whole picture. Martha spotted me straining outside my deck door, and she opened hers and asked what I was doing. I told her there was a 'snow heart' on the back of her chair, so she offered to go out and take the picture for me. That was the beginning of our special friendship. It wasn't long until I was sharing my heart-rock story with her.

Martha has a son who is in the Army, and at that time he was 1st. Lt. Bryan Cercy, and had recently returned from a tour in Afghanistan. Our church and many others faithfully prayed for Bryan, and we praised God for his safe return.

I love the military! I'm very proud and blessed to say I was raised in the Marine Corps. I know what our flag represents and what it stands for. I know our troops put their lives in harm's way for our peace and safety. I know their dedication, courage and sacrifices allow us to have the freedoms we enjoy and so oftentimes take for granted. And with that reality I'm reminded, once again, freedom is not free.

Martha, like me, also has a deep love for our troops and America. While Martha's son, Bryan, was deployed, she wanted our soldiers to have a little reminder of America; something they could carry in their pockets—something that would remind them of 'home' and that we, here in America, hadn't forgotten them. Martha had found a way she could keep busy, knowing her son was in harm's way—she made little 'pocket flags' and sent them to our troops. She included a little card with each flag that read...

A flag for your pocket so you can carry a little piece of home.
We are praying for you and we're proud of you.
Thank you for defending our country and our freedom!

Then one day Martha hollered over to me while I was on my deck. She said she had a mission she wanted to do for our soldiers. She wanted to send heart-rocks to our troops, a rock small enough they could carry in their pocket and hold in their hand as a reminder of God's love and protection for them. She then said she wanted these to reach the troops by July 4th. Well, that didn't leave much time, as we were already into the month of June. But God is good. We grabbed our buckets and headed out on a heart-rock mission. Within an hour we had nearly one hundred heart-rocks! Now remember, these rocks had to be small enough to go inside a little plastic bag that they could carry in their pocket. No easy feat to find this many rocks with just the correct size. But with God, we are reminded once again, all things are possible!

We washed the rocks before writing the scripture on them. On some we wrote Psalm 91, which is the prayer for protection.

God will place His angels around them
and He will be their fortress
where they can trust
and find security in Him for safety and rest.

On others we wrote Ephesians 6, which is putting on the "full armor of God" As our men and women in uniform are marching into dangerous territory, they could remember to depend upon the unlimited power of God to cover themselves with God's armor.

Martha printed up the little cards with the background of our beautiful American flag on them, along with this poem.

A heart-rock from America's land,
For you to hold bravely in your hand;
As a reminder of God's love for you,
You are a Hero for all that you do,
May God bless you and the Red, White and Blue!

"Colorado Supporting Our Troops" is an organization that puts together packages monthly to send overseas. They are filled with socks, toiletries, granola bars, etc. These are the packages we would add our heart-rocks to, but before we did that, we wanted them to be blessed.

I met with my Pastor and told him our plan of sending our troops heart-rocks. I asked if he would be willing to pray over them and bless them. He had a much better idea. He suggested Martha and I bring them to the Sunday service so the entire congregation could be a part of it. He actually wove the story into his sermon as well. Everywhere we turned, God was in this with us, blessing us in ways we never expected.

In Front of the TV Camera

Before we could get the rocks into the packages to be sent overseas, Martha called me and said we were going to be on TV to talk about our heart-rocks going to the troops! What? Are you kidding me? But God is always behind the scenes working out the details to bless His children.

So Martha and I were on **The Colorado Company Show**. It's a daily morning program that shares news and human interest stories about organizations and businesses. We had the heart-rocks in a beautiful basket with small American flags tucked in around them. Soon we would be on the air...live!

When it was my turn to be interviewed, I started to tell how it had all come to be that I find heart-rocks to bless others. I held up the heart-rock that I had found on the beach in Sitka, Alaska, so many years before. The host was astounded as she said, *"Yes, I see that is a perfect heart shaped rock. Did you make it? I mean did you carve it or grind it out of the stone?"* I had a huge smile on my face and said, *"No, I didn't make it. God did!"* I was on TV, talking about my Savior, and what He had done in my life, and how He is now blessing me to bless others.

I often think about our men and women who are in all parts of the world, putting their lives on the line for me, for all of us. I can't imagine the impact of what it must like to be so far away from home . . . to witness the horrible things their eyes see and their souls feel and how it all affects one's spirit negatively.

Soon our package was in the mail and it wasn't long until I received a letter from a deployed soldier who was blessed by his heart-rock. In part he said, *"Your heart-rock is truly moving, and I appreciate you sharing it with me. I have it prominently displayed in my room and get plenty of compliments and comments. You quickly find out who's a believer and who isn't."* He went on to say, *"I think it's important to make time for the finer things in one's mind, especially when in a war zone."*

After reading his letter my heart was overflowing with joy, praising God for using me as His vessel to minister and uplift the hearts and souls of our troops who endure the hardships of battle.

Another event I will always remember is when my husband and I went to a fundraiser for Colorado Supporting Our Troops sponsored by Water To Wine, a small winery that hosted this event often. I just loved the name of the place, as that was Jesus' first miracle—told in John 2, when He turned the water into wine.

Can you imagine my surprise when I learned we would be Skyping to a unit in Afghanistan where we had sent some of our rocks! I was overjoyed to have the honor of speaking with a soldier who thanked me personally for the heart-rock. Just to see his face, hear his voice and see the environment he was in was beyond words that I cannot describe.

When the word gets out that you're passing out heart-rocks, along with sharing the good news of Jesus, everyone wants one. One day I received a phone call from our Associate Pastor; he was going to conduct a wedding for a military couple who were both going to be deployed: the husband was going to Iraq and the wife to Afghanistan. He wanted to incorporate into their wedding ceremony, unbeknownst to them, a heart-rock that each could carry and be reminded of God's love. I loved the idea and the fact that our pastor was asking me for two heart-rocks!

I found two beautiful rocks (a white one for the bride) and wrote on them the scripture from the book of Genesis:

The Lord watch between me and thee
while we are absent from one another.
Genesis 31:49

I prayed over the rocks and I asked God to bless their marriage and to bring them home safely.

I love the uniqueness of God's wisdom in how He wants to use us to do His will. We were still living in Colorado, and my heart-rock ministry was continuing to grow in ways I could never imagine.

As I was leaving the nail salon one day, I was checking out the rocks and stones that were in the landscaping next to my car. I never pass up an opportunity to find a heart-rock, because in Colorado they are abundant. So here I am, bent over, looking at the rocks, and a lady comes over to me to tell me she just took a picture of my license plate. She said she loves to take pictures of people's clever personalized plates and she loved mine, which is GVAHUG (give a hug).

She asked if I had lost something in the rocks and I told her about my ministry with heart-rocks and how I find them and use them to share the love of Jesus. Well, she loved hearing that, because she was a Christian and involved with a women's ministry. She was pressed for time, but said she wanted to hear all about my story and asked for my phone number and she would be calling me.

Two years later I was outdoors watering the plants, and my husband came outside to say there was a lady on the phone who wanted to talk to me about my heart-rocks. I couldn't imagine who it could be, but took the call. It was the lady who had taken the picture of my license plate two years ago. Yes, two years ago! She said she had to go through all of her contacts in her phone before she finally found me, as she had forgotten my name. She wanted to invite me to her women's ministry meeting to share a little about my story.

Well, one thing led to another and before I knew it, I was asked to speak and share my story to the military wives at Buckley Air Force Base in Colorado. It was quite an evening, where I had the opportunity to personally speak with these women, some of whom were going to be deployed themselves, and to pray with them. All of them went home with a heart-rock.

America is the land that I love, down to the depths of my soul. I just love what President Ronald Regan said, *"If we ever forget that we are One Nation under God, then we will be a Nation gone under."*

With applause and deep admiration I salute our men and women in the military who are our brave 'warriors' for protecting and defending our nation, America, the beautiful!

~8~

Sharing Love from the Shepherd's Heart

Then I heard the voice of the Lord saying,
"Whom shall I send?" And I said, "Here I am. Send me!
Isaiah 6:8

How blessed I am to know God has given me the gift to share and witness His love for others through heart-rocks. Being the all-wise Creator, He has created them, just as He has uniquely created and designed each one of us. It has been amazing—the people I have met through my heart-rocks. There are many stories, too numerous to share in this book, that tell how these special rocks have blessed so many, but there are a few that resonate in my heart that I'd like to share.

My heart-rocks are an important part of my faith, and of who I am, for two reasons. First, God placed one in my path to draw me closer to Him when I had no hope. Not knowing it at the time, it was the beginning of my faith walk. Secondly, He knew that I, being an outgoing people person, would have the ability to use them to share the Good News of Jesus with others.

As Christians, scripture says we are to be the 'salt' and the 'light' of the earth. As salt is a preservative, we are to be different from people who do not know God. He wants us to be the salt in the stew of the people we encounter each day. We are to be the light in the world—to shine and not hide what we know to be true. A heart-rock is a fun and non-threatening way to plant the seeds of faith into the hearts of others, especially those who are going through the struggles of life. To be an encourager, to lift someone up and let them know they are loved and valued is part of the job description when you are a Christian.

I like to write the scripture from the book of Psalm 18:2 on the rocks when I give them away.

The Lord is my rock, my strength and my refuge.

We know that none of us are exempt from enduring some kind of pain along this life-journey on earth. Trials are bound to come, and it seems that we all get a turn at something in this life. Isn't that so true? At times we will walk through a deep and dark valley, but we have the assurance of a Shepherd who will provide for our every need. He is with us through our trials, giving us peace, strength, comfort, healing and love. "The Lord is my Shepherd, I shall not want." Having a heart-rock is a tangible reminder of His loving grace for us.

In addition to sending heart-rocks to our soldiers, I love to give them to my pilots whenever I fly. Remember, I'm not afraid to fly anymore! A little poem also accompanies their rocks. It says:

A heart-rock along for the ride,
A reminder that God's by your side;
For you and the crew and all that you do,
God bless you and the Red, White and Blue!

My husband prints up the little cards with the airline's logo on it, whatever airline we are flying. Mostly, we fly Southwest, whose logo happens to be a heart!

A few years ago, as I boarded the plane for a flight back from Sitka, Alaska, (where I had found my first heart-rock), I poked my head into the door of the cockpit and told the pilots I had something for them. I gave the rocks to the flight attendant who was at the door. She asked for my name and where I was sitting.

After we got to cruising altitude, a different flight attendant came back to me. She said all excitedly, *"I work up in First Class, and I saw what you gave the pilots. I'm a believer, too. Can I have a heart-rock? Do you have any more?"* I pointed up to the overhead compartment and told her my carry on was full of them. When we landed in Seattle, I waited for her to get off the plane, opened my suitcase and let her have her pick of the harvest. She couldn't believe the rocks I had in my bag. Sitka has wonderful heart-rocks! *(Later, I was thinking, goodness! Since she was working First Class, she might have at least brought me a glass of champagne in exchange for a heart-rock.)*

She did ask for my email, and we've kept in touch.

One November, Bill and I were flying to the east coast for our annual vacation in Cape Cod. As we were walking down the jetway, there was a pilot standing against the wall. I stopped and asked him if he was going to be our pilot. He said, *"Well, I'm going to be one of them."* I told him I had something for him and his partner. I gave him the heart-rocks, along with a short story about how God had changed my life by placing one in my path years ago, and that I'm not afraid to fly anymore. I told him they were reminders of God's love for him and that I wrote Psalm 91 on them, the prayer for protection. He grabbed me, gave me a hug and said, *"God bless you. I can't wait to see what God's got in store for you when you get to Heaven. I love Jesus, too, and I can't wait to share this with my partner. He's not a believer, and we're going to be in that cockpit for several hours. This is going to be fun!"*

On a trip to New York a few years ago, I knew I would be in Times Square for the TV show, Good Morning America. I love that show and watch it every morning and was wanting to give Robin Roberts a heart-rock. I've always admired her and knew she surely was a believer. I told the security guard at the door that I had something for Robin and I wasn't leaving until I could give it to her. When she came outside to mix with the audience, the security guard told her, *"This woman's been waiting a long time to see you and has something for you."* I gave her the rock and told her briefly about my ministry and that the rock would be a reminder of God's.love for her. She clutched it to her chest and said, *"You have no idea what this means to me."*

The following week she announced on the show she had been diagnosed with breast cancer. It was then that I remembered how she had clutched the rock to her chest and what she had said to me. I'm certain that was a God appointment. He knew Robin needed a heart-rock.

Making Contact with the Royal Couple

When Prince William and Kate Middleton made the announcement that they would be getting married on April 29, 2011, I was so excited. We were still living in Colorado at that time, and my girlfriend, Dee Getzinger, who attended our church, had a daughter who lived in London. Her daughter invited us to come over and stay with her during the time of this historic wedding. I had this vision of dancing in the streets and celebrating with all the other commoners, toasting and cheering on for the newlyweds. But my excitement was short-lived, when Dee took a fall during her morning walk six weeks before the wedding and broke her hip. I couldn't believe it. The most talked-about wedding around the world and I was going to miss it.

Ok, so I wasn't going to be dancing in the streets of London after all, but I would find another way to celebrate. I decided to have a Royal Wedding party. It started at 1:00 AM so we could watch the wedding take place live! I even had girlfriends who flew in from California for the event. I had a royal wedding cake, party favors for the girls and a framed picture of the Queen alongside Prince William and Kate. I made scones with clotted cream, chocolate covered strawberries and champagne. Many of the ladies wore 'fascinators', those stylish British hats. I wore a Swarovski tiara and the beautiful peignoir I wore on my wedding night when I married Bill.

I was thinking that Will and Kate would be showered with tons of gifts, but I was willing to bet that they wouldn't be getting any heart-rocks . . . that is, unless I send them one! So I found the most perfect heart-rocks for each of them and put them inside a beautiful organza bag with a drawstring. I found initials "W" and "K" made in rhinestones and attached them to each of the bags. I sent this, along with my story, and a small photo album of the pictures from my Royal Wedding Party.

Never in my wildest dreams did I expect to hear back from any of these people, so you can imagine my excitement when I went to the mailbox and there was a letter from Buckingham Palace addressed to me!

It read, "The Duke and Duchess of Cambridge thank you most sincerely for the photograph album and heart-shaped rocks, which you so generously sent to mark the occasion of their wedding."

I kept reading the letter, hoping that somewhere in there they would ask me to drop by the palace for high tea if I were ever in England.

No such luck, but how fun to get a royal letter in the mail from Buckingham Palace.

This scripture from Isaiah really ties into one of my favorite stories to share about the loving power and promise of God. God says,

> My Word shall not return to Me void,
> but it shall accomplish what I please,
> and it shall prosper in the thing for which I sent it.
> *Isaiah 55:11.*

Before our move to Colorado, a friend asked if I would send a heart-rock to an acquaintance of hers. This woman had gone through a horrible divorce, and was having problems with her adult son. She didn't know the Lord, and my friend thought sending her a heart-rock would be a good way to minister to her. I was more than happy to do that, so I mailed the rock, along with my little testimony, sharing with her what God had done for me in my life. I never heard back from this woman, and that was OK. I knew I had planted the seed . . . now it was up to God to water it.

I was a Spiritual Care Volunteer at our local hospital and I worked on the oncology floor. The volunteers were always given a daily roster of all the patients in the hospital. As I was looking over the list for my floor, a particular name caught my eye, because it was so unusual, and I knew I had heard it before. After pondering it for a while, the memory came flooding back to me—this was the woman I had mailed a heart-rock to a few years earlier.

I was so anxious to see her, so I decided she would be the first patient I saw that day. She was recovering from lung surgery. I went into her room and found her sitting in a chair near the window and I introduced myself to her.

She spoke in a whisper and said, *"I know who you are. You're the woman who sent me that rock."* I replied and said, *"Yes, I am."* She went on to say, *"When you mailed me that heart-rock along with your story, I thought to myself, 'how dare she try to preach to me about Jesus.'"*

I was taken aback and started to apologize profusely for offending her, but she kept on talking, and said, *"Please let me go on. I didn't know it then, but I realized I needed God in my life. He was the missing piece and now I have Him and I want to thank you and to ask for your forgiveness."*

Well, as joy washed over me, I told her there was absolutely nothing to forgive, because I knew all too well the path she had been on and I was blessed to hear her story and overjoyed to know she had accepted Jesus as her Lord and Savior! Then I prayed with her, thanking God for His Sovereign love for this woman.

Happiness doesn't come from the material possessions of this earth. Happiness comes when we are serving others, just as Jesus did when He walked on this earth. The Bible says,

Happy are the feet of those who preach the gospel of peace
who bring glad tidings of good things.
Romans 10:15

Well, there must be a reason God gave me size ten feet, because I'm sure putting them to good use as I share the love of Jesus with my heart-rocks!

~9~

More Rock Stories

As long as I live, I will forever carry in my heart the most wonderful Christmas present my husband gave to me on our first Christmas together.

I remember telling Bill not to get me anything, as I had everything I ever wanted or needed. My heart wanted to just celebrate us being together and to focus on the real meaning of Christmas—the birth of Jesus! He would smile and say. *"It will be our first Christmas as husband and wife, and so, of course I will be getting you just a little something."*

On that Christmas morning Bill handed me my gift. It wasn't a very large box, but it did have some weight to it, a little bit on the heavy side. As I was removing the ribbon, I was thinking about what it could be—a radio or perhaps a camera. The truth was, I didn't need either one of those items, but I proceeded to unwrap the paper. As I got down to removing the tissue paper inside, to my utter surprise, I saw a layer of heart-rocks neatly arranged in the box as if they were pieces of luscious See's candy.

I was stunned, overwhelmed, and touched by this gracious gift from my husband. I was speechless, and all I could do was cry. I cried because I was blessed with this affectionate and kind-hearted man who was now my husband. To know that he took the time to go to Dana Point and walk the beach to select for me the most perfect and priceless Christmas present was absolutely the most thoughtful gift for me.

Who needs diamond earrings and other jewelry when the right gift is the gift that truly comes from the heart and touches another's heart? It is an endearing treasure!

> Store up your treasures in heaven,
> for where your heart is,
> your treasure will be also.
> *Matthew 6:19*

I have never received another gift since that Christmas that came anywhere near to the unique, heartfelt and tenderness of that one-of-a-kind gift of heart-rock 'candies'.

> I am my beloveds, and he is mine.
> *Song of Solomon 6:3*

My youngest sister, Mary, has lived in Sitka, Alaska for over forty years. Sitka is a small community on the Baranof Island in southeastern Alaska. Whenever there is a tragic event, the entire town comes together, like a large and loving family, to mourn, to grieve, and to reach out in love in whatever way they can. Sadly, everyone is affected in some way whenever tragedy hits.

Mary always knew that she could count on me to pray for anyone, anytime, anywhere. One day she called to tell me about a horrific accident that resulted in the death of her friend's husband, and asked that I pray for this woman and her children.

The husband had been out at the shooting range with some other men, and when he didn't return home at the expected time, she became concerned. They were to be at their church for Mass, as was their custom each Saturday.

She tried to reach her husband by cell phone, but there was no answer. After several attempts of not reaching him, she decided to drive out to the shooting range to find out why he hadn't returned home.

As she drove down one of the main roads in this small community, she came upon stopped traffic and could see many police cars and flashing lights. She assumed it was a car accident, so she navigated through the traffic and continued on to the shooting range.

When she arrived at the shooting range, she was told there had been an accident. Unbeknownst to her, she had actually passed the truck that held her injured husband. He had been wearing a shoulder holster for his gun, and as he was placing the gun back into the holster, it went off, shooting him into his chest. The men at the shooting range had called for help and then placed her husband in the back of a truck, where they drove down to the main road to meet the first responders. Sadly, he passed away.

My sister and her husband went that night to offer comfort, not knowing what to say. But words don't really matter at a time like that—just show up and be there. That's what matters: just be there. Be a loving human; be present to cry, to hug, to pray; to reach out with your tears; and then let God do the rest.

After hearing this heart-wrenching story, I knew I needed to do something more than pray, although I know prayer is vital and important during times such as these. But my heart urged me to write to this woman, whom I had never met, and send her a heart-rock: a reminder of God's steadfast love for her during this sorrowful time.

About a month after the passing of her husband, I received a beautiful note from this woman. She thanked me for my 'kindness' and how it had touched her soul that a complete stranger would reach out to her to console and uplift her during a most painful time. It had left her speechless. She went on to say that she slept with the heart-rock in her hand and would carry it with her whenever she left the house, because it was such a tangible reminder of God, who was her Rock and her Savior. In closing, she said she would pray for me and my ministry.

I mention this to say that God has gifted each one of us to extend His love and compassion to others while we are here on this earth. We are to follow the example and pattern of Jesus, who God has given us as an example of what a human being is meant to be. God created us to be a community to reach out to others, not just to the people next door, but to anyone who needs to be shown the love and care of Christ, even in a tiny town as far away as Sitka, Alaska.

A couple of years later, I was blessed with the opportunity to meet this woman in person when I made a trip to Sitka to care for my sister's son. He had suffered a traumatic brain injury the year before, and Mary and her husband had been caregiving him 24/7. They needed some time away.

So it was on that trip that I was able to meet this woman who had lost her husband to that horrible accident. We met for lunch, hugged, prayed and really connected with one another. We went to a place called John Brown's Beach. It is on the Japonski Island where Sitka airport is located. The beach is literally below the runway at this small airport in Sitka. It is so beautiful, with lots of lush foliage, trees and indescribable beauty. We looked for heart-rocks and found a few. God is good!

It was there she told me about a story that had to do with finding pieces of blue sea glass and blue pottery. She told me she and her husband would go to John's Brown's Beach often to get away . . . just the two of them . . . because it was so serene and peaceful. It was their little oasis. During one of these outings, she took a picture of her husband sitting upon a large beautiful rock—his rock—at the place they always went. That was the picture she used for his obituary in the paper.

As their children grew up and left home, the 'empty nest syndrome' hit hard and she and her husband would go there to contemplate this new season in their lives. She told me her husband could always find blue sea glass or pieces of blue pottery, but she never could. Pieces of blue are very rare and hard to find, especially in Alaska, but he never seemed to have a problem spotting some.

As she journeyed through the process of grieving, (and it is a 'process', as everyone grieves on their own time schedule,) she yearned to know if her husband was at peace. She desperately longed to hear from him. She just had to know.

She told me she felt drawn one day to go to John Brown's Beach. She went to the sandy side of the beach and took a picture, because she was standing in the only space of sun behind her. Her shadow was bathed in light. It was like proof God was with her, and she was in His light. She wrote a message in the sand, telling her husband she loved and missed him.

She then said to her husband, *"I need to know you're at peace. I need some clarity. If you would just give me some blue glass to let me know you're at peace, it would help me so much. I'll know it's from you if it's at the base of your rock"*. As she walked over towards his rock, she said, *"I'd take a heart-rock too, but both, or either, would have to be TOTALLY obvious; I don't want to have to search for them."*

Before she even got to the front of the rock, she saw a giant piece of robin egg blue pottery, as blue as blue can be! You never find something that size and so pristine! The paint was beautifully intact, but old and weathered. As she circled back to leave, she was shocked by what else she saw. There, at the base of rock, on the west side, was a LARGE heart-rock, so clearly heart-shaped! It was braced against another rock and was so clearly a sign for her! What's strange is that, up close, the rock was chunky and one that a person would NEVER see as heart-shaped unless they saw it from that angle and braced as it was. It seemed clear to her that her husband was telling her he was at peace, and that now he wanted for her to be at peace, too. She said seeing that heart-rock was a connection to me because of the heart-rock I had sent her a few years earlier—her reminder of God's boundless love for her.

As the Apostle Paul wrote in his letter to the Corinthians,

But we have this treasure in clay jars,
so that it may be made clear that this extraordinary power
belongs to God and does not come from us."
2 Corinthians 24:7

We are all clay pots. We are breakable, vulnerable, and fragile. But God is the Master Potter and He shapes us to be beautiful vessels. God's love for us is boundless. Our God is a God who works wonders.

I spoke with this woman earlier this year, and she told me God had brought a wonderful man into her life, a godly man! I responded and said, *"You know that piece of blue pottery you found at the base of your husband's rock—the pottery you said*

106

was so pristine? I believe that was a message from heaven letting you know your beloved resides in a very pristine place...perfect, flawless, spotless . . . a place called heaven. But you're on this side of heaven and God wants you to be happy with the time you have here on earth."

God had, indeed, been weaving her 'safety net', thread by thread, and together we praised Him for second blessings of love!

I mentioned above that my sister's son had suffered a traumatic brain injury, and that I had gone to give her and her husband a break as caregivers. They had been told their son would not survive, so it is truly a miracle he is still with us today.

While I was there, different people would come by the house every few days to do physical and occupational therapy. It was during those times that I would head down to the beach with my bucket in hand to look for heart-rocks that I could bring home.

One day, the gentleman who did the physical therapy spotted my bucket sitting outside the front door. It was filled to the brim with heart-rocks. He was curious and asked me where they came from and what I was going to do with them. I thought, 'Here's another opportunity to share God's love', so I let him pick out the one he wanted.

About a month later, our mail carrier called me and said she had a package that was quite heavy and wanted to know if Bill was home; she said she would drive up our driveway to deliver it. She knew Bill ordered our salad dressing by the case from California because there were no stores that carried it in Colorado, so she was thinking it must be a double-order of salad dressing.

To my surprise, it was from Alaska. When I opened the box, I saw the biggest, most glorious heart-rock I had ever seen. There was no note—just the return address with the name of that therapist. I had put his phone number in my cell phone while I was up there so he could call me, if needed, while I was out to the store or down at the beach.

I excitedly called him right away to thank him for this amazing gift. He told me he was out in the forest hunting and when he came upon it; he just knew he wanted me to have it! I couldn't believe he didn't want to keep it for himself, but wanted to give it to me. I put this gorgeous rock on my bathroom scale and it weighed a hefty seventeen pounds! I laugh when I remember it was shipped in one of those Priority Mail boxes that you see on TV commercials: "If it fits, it ships". He really got a deal when he shipped that package. It graced my dining room for several years until we moved back to California.

That rock is now incorporated into
a fire-pit ring at my house.

I'll never forget the day my girlfriend and I met when we joined our church in Colorado. Dee Getzinger called to tell me something exciting. She was meeting another friend at a little restaurant in Littleton.

She noticed there was a man in uniform sitting in the next booth, and, because she loves the military as I do, she walked over to him and thanked him for his service. She said she always prays for the military, and that her church did, too! They started chatting, and he told her he was being deployed to Kuwait. His name was Captain David Nagel, a Chaplain at Buckley Air Force Base.

Dee had asked the chaplain if he and his family would like to come to our church to be blessed and prayed over before he left for his deployment, and he had said he loved the idea. He invited her to come out to the base, and Bill and I were invited too, because Dee knows how much I love the military!

What an exciting day that was for all of us. We were escorted onto the base and had a little get together in the Chaplain's office. I had brought a bucket of heart-rocks with me, knowing his children would be with him. Everyone selected the rock they wanted, including the Chaplain for his desk.

After we had a nice visit getting to know one another, Chaplain David took us on a private tour of the base. We toured the hangers and got to climb inside a Blackhawk helicopter! That was a sight to behold—I felt like we were inside the belly of a whale. (It made me think of the Bible story about Jonah and the whale.) Those helicopters are monstrous, huge pieces of equipment. I thought of the brave men who would ride in these helicopters and parachute to where they were needed to fight for the freedoms of others. So brave, so selfless, so giving.

Soon after that special visit, Dee and I met with our Pastor to discuss the idea, and we told him all about Chaplain David, who would soon be deployed to Kuwait. Our pastor said he would be honored to pray over this man and his family during our church service, so we set the date for this special event.

After the service, we had the Captain's family over to our house for a special barbeque. I decorated everything in red, white and blue.

During this time together, we were invited to the going-away and coming-home ceremonies for the troops at the Wings over the Rockies Museum! What a powerful time that was. The pageantry, the marching, the 'pomp and circumstance'—all that is involved to honor these men and women. It was hard to hold the tears back. When you see and witness a ceremony like this in person, it goes down deep into your soul. And then I'm reminded that freedom is not free! I am a proud American and LOVE our military.

Chaplain Nagel deployed with the 2-135th General Support Aviation Battalion in support of Operation Enduring Freedom in Kuwait. They had missions all over the Middle East during their time in the regions of Saudi Arabia, Jordan, United Arab Emirates, as well as a small contingent in Afghanistan. As chaplain for the group, he rotated throughout the mission areas, providing support. What a blessing to our men and women in uniform to have this man offer encouragement and comfort to those who were so far away from home.

Two years after returning stateside, Chaplain David was promoted to Major! To our unbelievable surprise, we were invited to that ceremony, and then to a wonderful reception afterward. Our God is so good, and we were blessed to share in these special, uplifting and memorable occasions. We will never forget Chaplain Major David Nagel and his family, the opportunity we had to pray together, and share in God's love, and to think it all happened because my girlfriend decided to have lunch in a little restaurant in Littleton, where he was eating, too.

While we were living in Colorado, it didn't take me long to share with all my neighbors my love for heart-rocks and the meaning behind them. One neighbor, Marcy McGeorge, really loved it, and went full steam-ahead starting a collection of her own. I told her that it seems God blessed that state abundantly by dumping these special stones so that you don't have to look far to find one. If you were to drive down her street today and look at the front of her house, you would know what I mean. From the top of the porch, going down to the walkway, each step is adorned with beautiful heart-rocks of all shapes, sizes and colors! God continues to multiply her collection.

Marcy was looking for a dermatologist one day, so I recommended mine. She called me after one of her appointments to tell me she had spotted a huge heart-rock outside of the office. It was a warm, sunny day and the office had the door propped opened using the rock. My neighbor went inside and told the lady at the front counter about it, and asked if she could have the rock. Marcy said she would go and find another large rock for them to hold the door open, but it would probably not be a heart-rock. For whatever reason, the lady said, *"No"*. This didn't sit well with Marcy, because she figured she could have just taken it without asking. Even though she was doing the right thing by asking, she couldn't believe she had been told No.

Shifting gears now for a moment in my story—all of the ladies at this office, along with my doctor, knew that I was a Christian, and they all knew about my love for heart-rocks. Because I had grown up on the beach my whole life with no sun block, I was now paying the price with several skin cancer surgeries, so I was a regular 'customer' there! When the time came for our move back to California, I made one final visit to get one more skin check, and to say goodbye to everyone.

After my examination, the doctor gave me a hug, and said she had a special gift for me. *"You will find it at the end of the hall sitting on the chair."* We said our goodbyes and I headed down the hall. There, sitting on the chair, was a big and very beautiful heart-rock! I was so excited that my doctor would do that for me. I couldn't wait to get the rock home and find a perfect spot on my patio to display it.

The next time my Marcy came over I said, *"You won't believe what my doctor gave me as a going away present."* I took her outside and pointed to the huge heart-rock. Well her eyes got as big as saucers, and her voice rose a few notches up, and she said, *"Hey, that's the rock I found that I was telling you about, and I even went into the office to ask if I could have it and the lady said, 'No'. That is my rock, Donna, not yours. I found it first."*

What could I say? I gave the rock back to her. After all, she was the rightful owner. But this is what I think happened — all the girls that worked in the office knew I was moving back to California, including my doctor. So when Marcy saw this one, and called their attention to it, I think the office girl went outside and got it so that the doctor could give to me for my going-away present. God works in mysterious ways, right?

But I knew how much Marcy loved that rock, so in my heart I knew it belonged to her, and I was happy to give it up with my blessings, because 'a friend loves at all times'. (Proverbs 17:17)

Once I became a Christian, it was my joy to share my story with others, especially those who didn't know Christ as their Lord and Savior. My family and friends knew this and so did my church family. There was a member at my church in Mission Viejo who had a sister, Lee, who lived in Chicago. Lee became a Christian at the age of forty-seven when her sister invited her to attend a Women's Retreat at Forest Home, in Forest Falls, California.

As you enter this Christian Conference Center, there is a sign that greets you. It says, 'Welcome to Forest Home, one mile closer to Heaven.' Anyone who has gone to Forest Home never leaves that mountain the same as when they arrived. It is a place where people of every age can hear the gospel, and lives are transformed. I knew it to be true, as I had attended that beautiful Christian Conference Center many times after becoming a Christian myself.

I didn't know Lee at the time, but her sister asked if I could send a heart-rock to Lee's husband. He was dying of cancer and didn't know Jesus, and her sister, who was now a Christian, wanted him to have salvation before he passed. She wanted the assurance that she would see him one day in heaven.

It was my joy to send this man a heart-rock and share with him my story. I wrote him a letter and told him how empty my life had been without Christ—that He was the missing piece, and that He was what I had needed. I told him that when you have Christ in your life, you have everything you need; you have peace, joy, hope, and the assurance of eternal life. I went on to say that everyone has the opportunity, up until the time they draw their last breath here on earth, to accept Jesus as their Lord and Savior. Her husband, in fact, did accept Jesus as his Lord and Savior before he passed away in 2000.

After the death of her husband, Lee moved to California and became a member of our church, and I finally got to meet this beautiful woman in person. She was a new Christian on fire for Jesus, and I could sure relate to that, as I was forty-four when I accepted Christ and loved to share with others what God had done in my life. When you become a 'born again' Christian, you are not the same person as you were before. Just like the Apostle Paul, when God removed the scales from his eyes, he became a new person who traveled to share and talk about Jesus.

Lee, like the Apostle Paul, wanted others to know what God had done in her life and to share the exciting journey she was now on. Lee was very involved with several different committees at our church, and everyone knew who this woman was. She influenced and inspired many. Sadly, Lee herself passed away at the age of fifty-six, due to cancer, but she was blessed to have nine wonderful years of knowing her Lord and Savior while she was here on earth. She died on April 7, 2004, just four years after her beloved husband.

I remember towards the end of her life when she came to church for the last time. She was in a wheelchair and people were lined up to hug, kiss and pray with her. Then it was my turn to spend a couple of precious minutes with this special lady. Despite her illness, she had that sweet smile and pure peace radiated from her face, because her heart was satisfied, and she knew where she was going. I didn't say goodbye to her; instead, I said, *"I'll see you later"*, because I know my final home will be in heaven one day.

On the day of her memorial service, the sanctuary was packed. Lee had touched so many lives with her joy and infectious spirit for Jesus. It was a beautiful, heartfelt service. We sang the song, Better Is One Day. Through our tears, we were reminded of the glorious transformation we take on when we pass from this home, earth, and journey upward into the presence of our precious Lord and Savior.

Then a tape was played, and to our surprise it was Lee speaking. It was her testimony of how God had filled her with the Holy Spirit and changed her life forever; she wanted everyone in that sanctuary to know it. You can only imagine how my heart skipped a beat when I heard my name mentioned in that tape.

Lee said, *"Donna Sprague sent my husband, who was not a Christian, a heart-rock and wrote him a letter of how God had changed her life. Because of that kind, simple gift, a rock that was a tangible reminder of God's love for us, my husband accepted Christ and now I know I will see him again one day in heaven."*

I was overwhelmed at hearing that, but I realized through my tears that I was doing what Christ had always put on my heart—to share the good news with others. How will people know if we don't tell them? We need to share with them that what we know is real. It's part of our job description as Christians, and we need to shout it from the rooftops. Christ came to die for us so that we will have a future with Him forever in heaven!

The Bible says that as Christians we are to grow in the grace and knowledge of our Lord and Savior and to allow Jesus to live His life in and through us. Lee did just that, for the nine glorious years she carried Christ in her heart and shared it with everyone she met!

* * * * *

* * * * *

* * * * *

* * * * *

* * * * *

* * * * *

Part 2

In My
Humble Opinion . . .

Things I Have Learned
and Now Believe

~10~

Prayer

Do not be anxious about anything,
but in everything, by prayer and thanksgiving,
present your requests to God.
And the peace of God, which transcends all understanding,
will guard your hearts and your minds in Jesus Christ.
Philippians 4: 6-7

This story has had twists and turns, mountains and valleys, highs and lows. I have been exhilarated, frustrated, discouraged, encouraged. But that's what Life is for each of is, isn't it? To take the long view of it, I realize that my love for Christ; my accepting him as my Savior; and my mission to share him everywhere I go—these have led me to achieve some viewpoints on Christian Living. I would like to share them with you, and, as I said above . . . in my humble opinion. I want to tell you about my thoughts on Prayer, Faith, Heaven, Blessings and Spiritual Gifts, about how they have affected my children . . . and some more heart-rock stories.

Prayer . . . What a beautiful gift we have been given from our Father in Heaven!

Prayer. . . It is my absolute favorite security blanket. I can wrap up in it, rejoice in it, rest in it and I oftentimes fall asleep in it.

My faith in Jesus and my prayer life are two of my deepest passions, and they're a part of my everyday existence. I love to pray; I depend on it daily to stay closely connected to God. What better way to rest in God's presence and tell Him I love Him!

Because of the journey God has brought me on and what He has done in my life, one of my favorite scriptures is this Psalm:

> I waited patiently for the Lord; he turned and heard my cry. He lifted me out of the slimy pit, out of the mud and mire; he set my feet on a rock and gave me a firm place to stand. He put a new song in my mouth, a hymn of praise to our God. Many will see and fear him and put their trust in the Lord.
> *Psalm 40:1-3*

That's what God did for me. He heard my cry. He rescued me. He gave me hope and He put a new song in my mouth. And my hymn of praise to our God is through prayer each and every day. I can't imagine starting my day without it. It's as important and getting up in the morning, showering and brushing my teeth. Today, prayer is in every facet of my life.

Prayer. What is it and how can we develop the habit of prayer? How can we recognize the importance of slowing down to pray and to listen to God? What is prayer? Listen to this beautiful definition from the book, **"The Language of Prayer."**

> *Prayer is so simple; it is like quietly opening a door and slipping into the very presence of God. There, in the stillness, to listen for His voice, perhaps in petition or only to listen, it matters not. Just to be there, in His presence, is prayer.*

The chief object of prayer, then, is to glorify God. Prayer is the most intimate communion we can have with Him. God loves us. He longs for us. He created us; we are His children; and He wants to hear from us. Through the Holy Spirit, God reveals Himself when we take the time to pray. Jeremiah 33:3 says,

> Call to Me and I will answer you and show you
> great and mighty things you do not know.

So, to stay connected to God, we need to depend on prayer.

Before becoming a Christian, prayer was alien to me. Because God was never a part of my life, neither was prayer. And because I was cut off from God's power, my life was overwhelming and I felt defeated. Well, I am living proof, and I'm here to tell you, nobody has to live a life like that!

Prayer is the key to unlocking God's power in your life. Prayer invites God to let His presence suffuse, to spread through our spirits, to let His will prevail in our lives. Prayer can water an arid soul, mend a broken heart and rebuild a weakened will. Prayer is our link to our Heavenly Father.

What a beautiful reminder that God never forgets us and we should never forget Him. Making prayer a habit is good insurance for your spiritual life. You never know when you'll need it, and you'll have the assurance of God that He is always taking care of you wherever you are.

Serving on the Prayer Team

I remember when I was asked years ago to be a part of the prayer team at our church, and to be available after the service to pray for others. I was still a fairly new Christian, only being on the journey for a couple of years. Knowing how others had prayed for me through the years, I was more than happy to give back to my church family. I joyfully and wholeheartedly accepted the assignment.

I will never forget that Sunday morning when I would be a part of the prayer team for the very first time. I said to my husband Bill, *"Today is the day I'm on the prayer team."* He said, *"Oh, that's right, today is the day."* I shot back and said, *"We'll pray that no one comes forward for prayer!"*

Bill said, *"Well, that's a fine way to serve the Lord."* To which I replied, *"I'm scared! I can't pray out loud for somebody else, especially when I don't know what they're going to ask me to pray for. I mean, if I knew what the situation was beforehand I could rehearse it and practice what I would say."* Bill laughed and tried to reassure me that I would be just fine and to remember that the Lord would be with me and He always provides. Ok, Bill. Easy for you to say!

As I sat through the service I couldn't even focus or enjoy the sermon that was being preached. My stomach was doing flip-flops; my heart was racing, and I had butterflies. Then the pastor gave the benediction and I knew I was up next!

As I stood nervously and looked out at the congregation leaving the sanctuary, I prayed that everyone would just leave. I said, *"Lord, why did I agree to do this? What was I thinking?"* I became very anxious and panicky. I was having what I like to call, a 'Moses moment'. I didn't want to do this. Send someone else, Lord. Then I spotted a woman heading right towards me and I knew there was no way out. This was it!

I started repeating in my head, the Lord provides, the Lord provides. Then I said, *"Father, be with me now and use me to be your instrument to comfort this person, help me to pray and please send Your Holy Spirit ASAP!"* And God, being the faithful and loving God that He is, did just that.

The woman approached me with tears in her eyes, as I listened to her pain. As it turns out, she was struggling with a similar situation I had gone through with one of my own children. I took her hands in mine and prayed. I know the Holy Spirit was with me that day, because I was amazed at the words that came flowing out of my mouth. God had sent the perfect person He knew I could comfort. Today, she and I are still very close friends. We share a kindred spirit and I think of the friendship I would have missed out on had I not been willing stretch myself and trust in the Lord. God knows our weakness in prayer and wants to help us. He loves to stretch our abilities and expand our potential. He is the one who can change our weakness into strength. So be open to that and allow God to stretch you. Adopt the Philippians Chapter 4 attitude:

I can do all things through Christ who strengthens me.

There are many reasons we are drawn to prayer. First, it is a wonderful way to fellowship and stay close to God. When we fellowship with God we find trust, confidence, peace, and joy in our lives as we grow in prayer.

We also know God's power flows through people who pray. When we fall to our knees and pour out our hearts to the Lord, we are surrounded by His presence and we feel a comfort and a peace we've never felt before. God enables us to get through the tough times. His power can change the circumstances and relationships in our lives when we immerse ourselves in prayer.

I will never forget when my husband was scheduled to have surgery at City of Hope for his prostate cancer. We had been recommended to go there by Dr. Nagasawa, an oncologist where we lived. I went outside to the parking lot, waiting for my dear friend, Lynn Sanchez, to arrive who would be staying with me during the surgery. My cell phone went off and I was expecting it would be Lynn telling me she was lost, because City of Hope is a very big and busy cancer hospital. To my surprise, it was Dr. Nagasawa calling. He wanted to let me know he knew Bill's surgery would be starting soon and that he would be praying for Bill and for a successful surgery.

Wow! I have never had a doctor call to tell me he would be praying. That was so reassuring and my heart was lightened, knowing God's presence was with Bill in that operating room.

Developing Good Spiritual Habits

Now that we know God invites us into His presence, how can we develop good 'spiritual habits'? We need to learn what disciplines are necessary for our prayer life and then practice these disciplines regularly.

To develop a good prayer life, we can go to the number one prayer expert, Jesus. Make prayer a habit. Jesus always had a regular time to pray, to fellowship with the Father. Although He had a busy ministry meeting the needs of many people, healing, preaching, and teaching—Jesus always found the time to pray with the Father. So to make prayer a habit, we need to make room for it in our daily schedule.

It would be no different if we wanted to learn how to play the piano or tennis or become a marathon runner—you would need to practice daily for you to become good at it. It's clearly stated in the Lord's Prayer when it says, "Give us this day, our daily bread." It doesn't say give us our weekly bread, or monthly or yearly bread. It says, 'daily'. So if prayer is to become a habit, a vital part of your life, you must have a regular time for it once a day, every day, without fail.

I would encourage you to go to the book of Psalms for inspiration. Psalms is the worship book, the prayer book for the people of God. From Psalms we can learn to pray with honesty and true humility. So pick out a Psalm and read or say it to God. You may feel clumsy at first, praying this way, but, like anything new, you will need to get disciplined and stretch yourself and work at it.

So make a daily appointment with God. He never forgets us, and we should never forget Him. When your daily life is anchored in prayer, it just becomes second nature. It's a part of who you are. You never have to worry or think about when you might need to use prayer—you just tap into the built-in reservoir of the living water.

Get away from distractions. Jesus often went away to pray alone, in solitude to spend time with the Father. Jesus tells us that when we pray, we are to go into our room and close the door and pray to our Father who is unseen. (Matthew 6:6) It's important to find a special place free from distractions where you can be alone with God. Just you and God, one on one.

How many times have you been in prayer when the phone starts to ring, the neighbor's dog is barking or you hear children playing outside? It's distracting and we can lose our concentration. So a private place insures a minimum of distractions. This can be a walk-in closet, a corner in an office, a laundry room or even a workshop out in the garage. Wherever you find it, make it your special 'holy' place where you meet with God daily.

When my husband's job transferred us to Colorado twelve years ago, there were many things to learn about and to explore. One huge blessing was that every house in Colorado has a basement! Little did I know at the time that Colorado also has tornadoes. It wasn't too long before a special part of our basement would become my 'prayer room'.

The tornado siren was situated on our street just a couple of houses away. The first time that siren went off (and was it ever loud!) a man's voice came on the speaker and said, *"Go to your basement immediately, and take cover"*. Bill and I ran down to a part of our basement that was an alcove about four feet wide with three-sided concrete walls. We prayed and held on to each other as we listened to the siren overhead until the storm had passed.

I then realized that it was a perfect spot to pray. It was small, intimate, and protected. Bill even cut a nice piece of carpet to put inside, and I hung crosses on all three walls. I loved decorating my prayer room. I had my own little chapel within my home. I could go there any time I wanted to spend time alone with God. I even had a kneeling prayer bench!

When we moved back to California from Colorado, our house had no basement, so I made my walk-in closet my 'War Room', from the movie with the same title. I had a white erase board that was attached to the back of the closet door, where I had the names of people I prayed for each day, organized under different categories.

Be creative and you, too, will find that special place where you can be still and rest in God's Holy presence through prayer.

Pray from your heart. God is not impressed with fancy words or phrases. Just talk to Him as you would a friend. Tell Him how you feel or what you're worried about. Be honest with Him. He can handle it. Besides, He already knows what you need before you even ask Him.

Pour out your hearts to Him.
Psalm 62:8

Remember, He loves just plain, simple, exciting you! Don't feel intimidated. When you bond your heart with His, you are in perfect prayer.

Pray with faith. Jesus said, "I tell you the truth, if you have faith and do not doubt, you can say to this mountain, 'Go throw yourself into the sea' and it will be done. If you believe, you will receive whatever you ask in prayer." Jesus was referring to the mountain figuratively, but in today's world, we all face obstacles and roadblocks in our lives. As believers, when we pray through faith, we have confidence that God will remove that 'mountain', that obstacle or that roadblock. Faith comes from looking at God, not the 'mountain', so keep your focus on Him.

Remember, developing prayer fitness is like developing physical fitness; to stay in balance, you need to have a routine. A life with prayer is exciting and stretching.

I can't imagine starting my day without spending time with God in prayer. Our spiritual bodies, like our fleshly bodies, need daily food. The Bible tells us our physical bodies are going to waste away . . . they are just our earthly tents. So doesn't it make sense that our spiritual bodies be given the highest priority of maintenance?

Feed upon God's word, for it's the nourishment for our souls, and make prayer the "heartbeat" of your spiritual body. After all, that's the body that really matters. For that's the body that will live forever!

I've been subscribing to Guideposts ever since I became a Christian and I know reading other people's stories has helped to deepen the roots of my faith. I have never forgotten some stories I've read, and often have shared them with others. Here is one in particular that I will always remember.

A woman was placed in an assisted-living home after Alzheimer's made it impossible for her to care for herself. Her daughter received a call one day from the supervisor, saying her mother had been taking small things from other people's rooms: socks, candy bars, etc., but this time someone's silver cross was missing. After questioning her mother, the daughter found the cross and returned it, apologizing profusely. The supervisor said, *"Oh please don't. It's ok. Your mom is just trying to hang on to the things that mean the most to her."*

On the next visit the daughter brought her mother a small silver cross. Eventually, the mother was placed in a facility where she could receive more care. She adapted quite well, to the point where she even led prayers on Friday morning. Although Alzheimer's had robbed her mind of almost everything else, the prayers came to her lips as if she had freshly committed them to memory.

What a beautiful reminder that God never forgets us and we should never forget Him. Making prayer a habit is good insurance for your spiritual life. You never know when you'll need it and you'll have assurance from God that He's always taking care of you wherever you are.

Slow down to pray. It's important to find time for quiet moments with God. We all have busy lifestyles today, with cell phones, pagers, beeper, faxes and emails to answer—the list goes on . . . not to mention our families, household responsibilities and jobs. But if we want our walk with Christ to be growing and maturing, we need to slow down the pace. We need to reclaim our time. You can't build any kind of relationship when you're on the go. To get to know someone, you have to slow down and spend time together. We make time in our lives for the people we love so we should give God that same priority.

Many years ago, the Crystal Cathedral hosted a Conference for Care and Kindness. I had the privilege of attending many of these conferences, where I developed better skills on how to extend God's love to others.

At the conference I attended in 2006, I had the privilege of meeting Dr. Siang-Yang Tan, who was one of the keynote speakers. Dr. Tan is the senior pastor of First Evangelical

Church in Glendale and serves on the Board and Ministry Team of 'Renovare', a spiritual renewal ministry. This man truly had a heart for Christ.

In his book, **Full Service, Moving from Self-Serve Christianity to Total Servanthood**, Dr. Tan emphasizes that Jesus has called us first to servanthood as His disciples. We serve the Lord as our audience of 'one'.

Dr. Tan says we can learn a lot from our Master Servant, Jesus, who wants us to follow Him all the way, every day, because Jesus is our best friend. Remember those initials: WWJD, What Would Jesus Do? They can also stand for Walk With Jesus Daily. We can walk with Jesus daily by spending time with Him in prayer, solitude and silence. This is deep fellowship with our best friend and it cannot be rushed or hurried. It is about abiding in Christ or remaining in friendship and communion with Him, thereby bearing much fruit. Without Jesus—apart from Him—we can do nothing!

I'm remembering the day I was leaving the grocery store and I noticed a woman trying to maneuver her shopping cart. She had a terrible limp and looked like she was in a lot of pain. It was like God spoke to me and said, *"Donna, this one's for you. She needs your help and comfort today. Give her Jesus."*

As I approached her, I could see her leg was very red and swollen. I offered to help unload her groceries as she told me she had cellulitis, a very serious infection. I told her I, too, had suffered from cellulitis a few years ago, so I could identify with her pain. She then said to me, *"You're a Christian, aren't you?"* I said, *"Yes, I am."* She said, *"I knew it, I knew it."* She burst into tears as she told me she had lost her job and was going to an interview in a couple of days.

It just seemed so natural for me to ask her if I could pray for her. She welcomed it immediately. So there we were, in the middle of the parking lot of Albertson's in broad daylight, praying for God's healing and comfort. I felt so blessed that God had placed this lady in my path that day to offer her comfort and encouragement.

~11~

Faith

*Now faith is being sure of what we hope for
and certain of what we do not see.
Hebrews 11:1*

Like ***Much-Afraid***, as she journeyed along her spiritual path collecting her rocks and trusting Jesus more each day, I, too, had been given the seed of hope and love from Jesus. I was taking tiny steps along with a small leap of faith, not really knowing what Jesus had in store for me. But I knew something profound was happening within my soul, and so I continued on my new journey, not wanting to ever look or go back to the life I once had.

Going to church, reading my Bible, joining a Bible Study and praying each day, these were all vital—they played an important role in my faith journey. There was still much I didn't understand about God and His son Jesus, but I knew that was OK. We don't need to know everything about God and His mysterious ways, because if we did, we wouldn't need Him; we would desire to become our own god, thinking we knew what would be best for our lives and doing it our own way. But Jesus longs for us to seek Him, to follow Him and to trust in Him, and that was what I knew I wanted to do. Not understanding all that's in the Bible was OK, as long as I trusted and believed in what God's word said.

139

When I was a new Christian, I would always cry in church whenever we sang **Great is Thy Faithfulness,** about how . . .

Thou changest not
Thy compassions they fail not
. . .
Morning by morning new mercies I see
And all I have needed Thy hand hath provided
Great is Thy faithfulness
Lord unto me

Looking back, memories would flood my mind as I remembered all the ways God had provided for me during my darkest times. Even today, tears of utter joy and gratitude fill my heart whenever that beautiful hymn is sung.

When we want to learn more about faith, we can go to the book of Hebrews chapter 11. We can sink our spiritual roots deep into God's word when we remember Jesus is the author and finisher of our faith. We can believe it, even if we don't understand it. Our faith will grow and deepen when we trust in God's love through the gift of His son, Jesus.

We can look back and reflect on the history of the Old Testament and see how faith was modeled by Moses, Noah, Abraham and Sarah. They believed in God and trusted in something that was unseen, and yet they put their faithfulness to the test. What beautiful stories to encourage us to press on and grow in our faith.

Being a Christian doesn't make you exempt from facing adversities in your life. Trials are bound to come, and it seems we all get a turn at something in this life. Isn't that so true? Nowhere in the Bible does it say you will not face struggles just because you follow Jesus. In fact, the Bible tells us, through the words of Jesus, "In this world you will have trouble." Joys and sorrows seem to be intermingled because we live in a broken and flawed world, and God seems to get the blame for all the evil and bad things that happen. But God is not the one to blame, for God is good.

The difference between a Christian and a non-believer is that Christians have hope. We have the assurance of a Shepherd who will provide for our every need. Jesus is with us through our trials, giving us peace, strength, comfort, healing and love. The Lord is my Shepherd, I shall not want. Jesus has overcome the world. Faith is having the perception of what the future will be.

We also have the gift of the Holy Spirit, our Friend and Companion. The Holy Spirit is like oxygen for our souls. Even though you can't see it, we sure do believe in oxygen for our physical bodies, right? So it is with the Holy Spirit for our spiritual bodies. Even though we can't see Him, we can certainly trust in Jesus and believe in Him.

When we bring our problems to the Lord and invite Him into our daily life, we will experience His power wherever our day takes us. Jesus tells us:

> Surely I am with you always, to the very end of the age
> *Matthew 28*

We deepen our faith when we feed upon God's word through the Bible, knowing we are connected to His spirit. We grow in so many ways when we share fellowship with other believers, knowing we are rejoicing and praising Jesus in an intimate way. We journey through this world together as pilgrims onward towards heaven.

Jesus tells us:

> I am the vine, you are the branches.
> He who abides in Me, and I in him, bears much fruit;
> for without Me you can do nothing.
> *John 15:5*

So Jesus, in His tender way, cuts off any branch that does not bear good fruit. He prunes us so we can grow stronger and be obedient to do whatever He calls us to do. We abide in Jesus because we love Him, and our faith is how we live our lives day-to-day, fulfilling His purpose for us.

Faith is not only our hope for our eternal future, but for our lives as we live each day out here on earth. When we embrace our faith, we have better health. Scientific research has shown that people who attend church and pray regularly have lower death rates, and are less prone to depression, suicide, and other addictions. Faith connects us to other believers who are there for us when we need them. Through faith, our stress levels are lowered, and we have peace that God is always with us.

These thoughts, then, are among the things I have learned:

- Live your life in such a way that others will see and want what you have.

- Share your faith and tell them about Jesus.

- Be the salt and light of the earth.

- Make a difference in the lives of others who do not know God.

- Let your faith show others that you are different, that you live your life for Jesus!

When my husband suffered pulmonary embolisms six years ago, the doctors at the hospital were recommending a procedure that carried some serious risks. Before they wheeled Bill into the operating room, I was asked if I was ready to say good-bye to my husband, I told the doctor, *"Yes, but first I want to pray over my husband."* The doctor said, *"I think that is a wonderful thing to do."* I watched as the doctor took Bill's hands in his and all the nurses gathered around and placed their hands upon my husband. Then I prayed for God to bless the doctor and everyone who would be participating in the procedure and to watch over Bill and restore him back to good health. When Bill was wheeled away, I went to the chapel in the hospital and fell on bended knee and continued to stay close to the One I knew was in control. God heard my prayer and Bill recovered just fine. Praise God from whom all blessings flow!

This is just one of so many stories I can share to let you know I could not have gotten through the storms of life without my faith and the gift of prayer.

Delight yourself in the Lord,
and He shall give you the desires of your heart.
Psalm 37:4

When we delight in Jesus through our faith we don't have to freak out or worry in times of troubles. Our hearts bond with His and we have exquisite joy as the desires of our hearts are filled with the richest of God's blessings. Our hearts are satisfied.

My collection of heart-rocks continued to grow, and I always sang praises to Jesus for each and every one He placed in my path for I trusted He had a plan for them as well.

Anyone who knows me knows that I love Jesus and I want to share that love with anyone God puts in my path. Giving a heart-rock to someone, especially a total stranger, not knowing if they are a follower of Christ, is utter joy for me.

While we were in Colorado, we had Terminix for insect control. I'll never forget the day the doorbell rang; it was a new gentleman who would be doing the service. I had a nice attractive arrangement of heart-rocks on our front porch and when I opened the door, this man made a comment by saying, *"I love those heart-shaped rocks."* I told him I was a Christian and used them in my ministry to share God's love with others. He was a very shy, quiet man, a man of few words, but he did say softly, *"Well, I'm a believer too."* I said, *"Well, that's great"*. I told him a little bit about how God worked in my life through a heart-rock.

While he was outside spraying, I went into my garage and got a manly-looking heart-rock out of my collection to give him. I also printed out a copy of my little heart-rocks sermonette I had shared at church a few years earlier. When he rang the bell again for me to sign the invoice, I presented him with the rock and my story. He thanked me quietly for the gift and left.

Three months later, the Terminix man returned for our regular service. After I had signed the invoice and he was about to leave, he stopped, turned around and said, *"I want to thank you for the heart-rock and your story. I believe in Jesus but don't wear my faith on my sleeve, so it's hard for me to share with others. But I put your heart-rock on top of my Bible on the coffee table and now people have been asking me about the heart-shaped rock. Your heart-rock has opened the door to help me share the love of Jesus with my friends and I want to thank you so much for giving me one."* My heart was jumping for joy! When we can be bold and share our faith with others, we are encouraging them to do the same.

After I transferred from Mission Viejo High School as the Attendance Clerk to the district office, I worked in Child Care Division, a part of the Recreation Department. Our division provided onsite child care at all our elementary schools. (This was before and after school child care for working parents.) We often would hire high school students who had class schedules that allowed them to be off in the afternoon.

Brian Eaves, a former student at Mission Viejo High School, was one of the Supervisors. He is a Christian, and he knew I was one, too.

One afternoon Brian was interviewing the high school students for the position of Child Care Leaders. They would work with the children and help to watch over them while on the playground.

I'll never forget the day Brian called and asked that I come into his office. He told me to have a seat, and then proceeded with this story. He said to me, *"Did you see that kid that just left? I want to tell you a about the interview. You're going to love this one, Donna"*.

Brian went on to tell me that he had posed this question to the young man, *"If you were out on the playground with a group of children and you realized one was missing, what would you do?"* The young man thought for a moment and then responded and said, *"Well, in the Bible, Jesus says, if a man has a hundred sheep and one of them goes astray, does not he leave the ninety-nine and go seek the one that is straying?"* So he said he would leave the children and go searching for the lost one.

I said, *"Oh, Brian, how precious is that? That was the right answer wasn't it?"* Brian responded with a resounding, *"No, that is not the right answer! You would never leave a group of children to go looking for one that was missing! You would use*

145

your walkie-talkie and call for someone to go look for the missing child."

I argued back and said, *"But how was he to know he would even have a walkie-talkie? Plus, he was quoting Jesus, and that has to count for something. Right? You gave him the job, didn't you? Please say that you did."* Brian was laughing and said, *"Of course Donna. Don't worry. He got the job!"*

I was so impressed this young man knew the Word of God and that he answered from his faithful heart, knowing Jesus wants all of his children saved.

My Two Children

Now that I had salvation, I wanted that for my children as well. I wanted to see my children in heaven one day, where we would live together eternally. I prayed unceasingly for many years that my daughter and son would come to know Jesus. I didn't even know where my son was, as we had been estranged for many years. Was he dead or alive? I had no idea, but I knew Jesus knew all about my son, whether I did or not, and that was enough to give me peace, comfort and hope. The Lord hears the prayers of a mother's heart.

One day I received an email from my daughter, Heather. She told me she knew I was into religion, but she was not. My daughter told me she would never become a Christian because she just didn't believe in it. So what's a mother to do? I just prayed harder and fervently.

About a year later, I received an email, and in it she told me so beautifully how she had become a Christian. In part she said, *"It's not that I decided to become a Christian, but rather, when I decided to open my heart, there was no other option. There really wasn't a choice to make.*

146

It is something you could never explain to someone who isn't there. I know you know exactly what I mean. I know I have a lot to learn; and I'm excited to be on this journey. I want to thank you for sharing with me what you know about Jesus. I love you!"

Now, if that weren't enough for a mother to shout about, there was more to come!

My son, Aaron, was not in my life and he was following a path that held no future for him. We were out of touch for several years, and I would hear just snippets here and there from other relatives about where he was and what he was doing. But I am a prayer warrior and believe in the power of prayer. Every morning I prayed and asked Jesus to place another Christian in his path that would extend His love to him and give my son a glimmer of hope.

Then one day my son called. It was the first time he actually sounded like his old self—we had a good conversation. He told me he was working really hard and trying to get his life back on track. I told him that's what I prayed for him every day.

My son responded and said, *"Hey Mom, the neatest thing happened to me at work today."* He was living out of state and was working as a butcher at a grocery store. He went on to say that a lady said the nicest thing that anybody had ever said to him. Well, my curiosity was certainly up because he was so excited about the whole thing.

This is what he told me. *"Mom, I was at the counter and this lady came up and was checking out the different cuts of meat. She looked up at me and said, 'Smile'. I mumbled and hung my head down. She again said, 'Smile, Jesus loves you.' I told her,*

'Well, He's the only one that does.' *She replied,* 'And He's the only one that matters!' "

My son said it really made him feel good. I told him I prayed for him every day, and that I always asked God to place a Christian in his path who would show the love of Jesus. He replied, *"Well, that must have been the lady Jesus was sending me."*

My heart was so full of joy knowing Jesus had planted a tiny seed in the soil of my son's heart. Then I prayed daily that God would water and cultivate it. And water and cultivate it, Jesus did!

Now after many years of no contact with my son, my daughter called and said she wanted me to come over—that Aaron wanted to see me. He was in a good place. Feeling a little uneasy and as to how the visit would go, I prayed and knew Jesus would be in the midst of us. I had nothing to fear. There were lots of hugs and I love you's and then my son said, *"Hey Mom, guess what I did?"* I couldn't wait to hear what he wanted to tell me. With a huge smile on his face, he said, *"I got baptized!"* What, you got baptized? He said, *"Yes, full immersion in the ocean."*

My son has been an avid surfer since he was about nine years old, surfing every weekend. So this is how he explained the wonderful event of his baptism.

He was out surfing and saw lots of people getting baptized in the ocean. So he got in line and crashed the baptism, saying that he, too, wanted to be baptized. The pastor told him to go and wait up on the beach—that this wasn't how they did it, and he would talk with him in a while.

The pastor told my son what baptism meant, accepting and following Jesus and that being baptized was not a free ticket to heaven. My son agreed and said he knew it meant having an intimate relationship with Jesus, and that this was something that was missing in his life and he wanted and needed it. So, out into the ocean they went and my prodigal son was baptized in the water he loves and where he surfs every day . . . the ocean that God created so many years ago. I can't tell you how happy this made me and how his story filled my heart with joy and the confirmation of God's love for us.

I know Jesus hears every prayer. We just don't know when our prayers will be answered. But, they will be . . . in His time . . . for He's the one in control, and He knows the plan He has for us.

~12~

Heaven

No eye has seen, no ear has heard,
No mind has conceived what God has prepared
for those who love him.
1 Corinthians 2:9

Heaven! Isn't it a beautiful word? Did you know the life to come is more 'real' than the life we now have here on earth? I deeply believe, down to the depths of my soul, that this is true, because I believe in the Bible and what Scripture has to say about the promise of eternal life. I believe that Jesus was a human being that walked on this earth, teaching, preaching, healing and bringing hope to those who would believe and follow Him. I believe He died and rose again, and through His resurrection we have the priceless gift of heaven, our eternal home.

Heaven will be a place of joyous celebration, where there will be no more tears, pain or sorrows. I have the greatest hope through Jesus, knowing that one day I will be with Him in Heaven. It's something I hang on to and look forward to as I journey through this life on earth, sometimes with twists and turns that only draw me closer to Jesus. Knowing this place here on earth is not my permanent home, it gives me something to look forward to. The best is yet to come. I can live a non-anxious life because I have Jesus and His grace.

Every day when the sun comes up, we are one day closer to death. It's a fact — it's inevitable. One day we will all face death, whether we like it or not; it's going to happen. As I mentioned earlier, statistics show that ten out of ten people will die. We will all face a 'physical' death, but the good news is, we don't have to face a 'spiritual' death. We have a hope for our eternal future through Jesus Christ if we only believe that He took our place on the cross and died for us. We need to be prepared to die for the life to come.

Therefore we do not lose heart.
Though outwardly we are wasting away,
yet inwardly we are being renewed day by day.
For our light and momentary troubles are achieving for us
an eternal glory that far outweighs them all.
So we fix our eyes not on what is seen, but on what is unseen.
For what is seen is temporary,
but what is unseen is eternal.
2 Corinthians 4:16-18

Through our death, when we shed our earthly 'tent', we have a building from God, an eternal house in heaven, not one built by human hands. When we live in Christ, we don't have to be afraid to die, because we have the promise that our soul lives forever!

Jesus said,

I am the resurrection and the life.
He who believes in me will live, even though he dies;
and whoever lives and believes in me will never die.
Do you believe this?
John 11:25

I certainly believe this with all my heart. Don't waste time struggling to understand and trying to figure it all out. Forget the intellect part. It's not head-knowledge that gets you into heaven, but heart-knowledge. There's much we will never understand about God's mysterious ways. But when we open our heart and invite Jesus in, we have God's blessed assurance that we will live in our heavenly body forever in His kingdom. Take a leap of faith—trust in God's word and His promises.

I am remembering a very special friend and neighbor who became ill with a fatal disease. As soon as I heard the news, I was praying for her and asking God for His healing to be upon her. Next, I gave her a heart-rock and shared my Reader's Digest version with her. With every additional hospital stay, she took her heart-rock with her.

She called one day from the hospital to let me know that they had moved her to another room. She didn't miss a beat, and told me she made sure her rock was with her, because she wanted the constant reminder that Jesus was with her, too. She told me she shared that rock with every doctor, nurse and technician who came into her room. I told her I was proud of her, and how she had turned her hospital bed into a pulpit, sharing the promises of Jesus with so many. She was planting the seeds of hope into the hearts of others, not knowing if they embraced a faith or not.

While my husband and I were on vacation, I'll never forget the day she called to tell me she was going home. I was so excited for her because it meant she had turned a corner and was getting better. I asked her when they were discharging her from the hospital and going home. That's when she set the record straight and said, *"I'm not going home—to my house. I'm going home to my real home—heaven."* Before I could take it all in and respond, she asked me to tell her what I knew about heaven. As sick as she was, with her voice just a whisper, she said she was excited to know.

I knew in that moment God had blessed me with the right words and scripture to share with her to bring hope and reassurance of the promise we have in Jesus. I told her there was nothing to be afraid of because,

To be absent from the body is to be present with the Lord.
2 Corinthians 5:8

So when we die, we get the greatest gift of being with Christ forever in heaven, knowing our bodies will be changed into glorious bodies like His own.

Before we hung up, I prayed and told her I loved her. She said, *"I love you, too, and I'll see you in heaven."* A couple of hours later, I received a phone call from her sister telling me my friend and neighbor was now home in heaven, and she thanked me for having the conversation that was a comfort and a blessing to her sister.

I read a wonderful book called, **Glimpses of Heaven, True Stories of Hope & Peace at the End of Life's Journey**. It was written by a nurse who had worked in hospice care for twenty-two years. She had witnessed glimpses of heaven countless times through the lives and deaths of her patients.

Patients would tell her they had visions of loved ones who had gone before them. They spoke of angels more beautiful than they had ever imagined, and music more exquisite than any symphony they had ever heard. They mentioned colors too beautiful to describe. The author said that in some inexplicable way that we do not yet understand, they seem to travel back and forth from this world to the next, developing the insights God wants them to have on their final journey back to the Father who created them.

It seems God finds a way to lighten our fears and burdens at the time of leaving this world. We have faith in realizing that dying is the path to a new life. We do not lose the ones we love, they only go before. Heaven is our reward. The promise of heaven brings us hope today and hope for our tomorrows. Through the death and resurrection of Jesus, we have the assurance that

Nothing, absolutely nothing,
will ever be able to separate us from the love of God.
Romans 8:39

In this world today, it seems like everyone is focusing on the wrong things. It's so easy to get caught up in the materialism, when that's all we're surrounded with every day through the television, newspapers and magazines. But driving fancy cars, wearing designer clothing and making a lot of money is not what you need to prepare for your eternal future. You need Jesus. You need to get ready and be prepared for the life that is to come. The life that really matters has nothing to do with the things of this earth.

There is a scripture that really puts the above paragraph into perspective:

Do not store up for yourselves treasures on earth,
where moth and rust destroy,
and where thieves break in and steal.
But store up for yourselves treasures in heaven,
where moth and rust do not destroy
and where thieves do not break in and steal.
For where your treasure is, there your heart will be also.
Matthew 6:19

Make Jesus your number one treasure. Take up your cross and follow Him, love Him, abide in Him and praise Him. Thank Him for all He has done for you, and when you do, you will have treasures of heaven stored up in your heart.

We know through scripture that the gift of heaven is available to every person on earth. Yes, we will endure sickness, disease, and ultimately, death, for all are a part of living on earth. But this earth is not our permanent home—we are just all passing through. For as a believer in Christ, I know my permanent citizenship will be in heaven. We can look forward to a home yet to come. (Hebrews13:14)

God gives us the gift of free will, the freedom to choose. You can choose Jesus or not. I choose Jesus each and every day because I know and believe in my heart He is the Son of God, and I need Him to get through this life here on earth, until I am with Him one day in heaven.

And on that day, when my mansion is complete and I'm called 'home', I will humble myself and, if I am worthy, I will hear my Lord say, "Well done, good and faithful servant; now enter into the joy of your Lord."

~13~

Blessings

As Christians, we are all called to be disciples of Christ, to reach out to others with the love of Jesus. It is part of our job description. Jesus said,

Take care of my sheep.
John 21:16.

Be prepared and obedient to share what you know about the gospel. Be bold, brave and courageous, knowing God is always with you and He will work through you. The more we reach out to others, blessings come back ten-fold.

Ministering with heart-rocks is a mission God has placed on my heart and it is a fun, non-threatening way to share the 'good news'—and who wouldn't want a heart-rock? Plus, they're so much fun to use as decoration. I have them on my front porch, back deck, in my shower, my car, widow-sills, and I always carry one in my purse. They make great door stops and paper weights, too. I find them everywhere . . . at the beach, the desert, the mountains, restaurants, hospitals, Costco and even Target. God has seasoned the earth with these special rocks, literally everywhere.

God oftentimes surprises me in unexpected ways with messages of His love, other than in a heart-rock. A heart cloud, a heart shaped potato chip, a heart puddle after a rain, even a snow heart. I see hearts all over the place—another reminder that God's love is everywhere!

My husband and I were attending our grandson's cross country track meet a few years ago. Not wanting to wait for the shuttle for fear of missing his race, we decided to walk the mile and a half to the event at a very brisk pace. Thankfully, we got there in time and saw the race. Walking on the way back to where the team was meeting, Bill said, *"I'm pretty sure I have a blister."* I replied, *"Oh, that's just great. You're on Coumadin, so I hope it didn't pop or you could be in trouble."* He sat down, pulled off his shoe and I removed his sock. I said, *"Bill, You're not going to believe this. You definitely have a blister, it's a blood blister and it's in the shape of a HEART!"* His daughter didn't believe me until I swung his leg around and she about fell over. Well, that's our God—full of love and surprises in some of the most unusual ways!

Today my heart-rock collection totals in the hundreds, if not thousands, and God continues to place them abundantly in my path, proving that God is not into addition; He's into multiplication! You cannot outgive Him, no matter how hard you try. He's an extravagant God and my cup truly overflows.

For my fiftieth birthday, back in 1998, Bill took me on a cruise that included going to Israel. I was a new Christian back then, taking 'baby steps' and on fire for Jesus. I still am! I couldn't wait to see the Jordan River where Jesus was baptized; Capernaum, where He shared God's word and healed many people; and the Garden of Gethsemane, where He prayed the night before He was crucified. I was especially excited to see the Sea of Galilee, where Jesus walked, preached, and met with the fishermen, telling them to drop their nets and follow Him and He would make them fishers of men. I told Bill I was hoping I could find a heart-rock, maybe even one that Jesus' dusty sandal had walked upon. That's what I was hoping and praying for.

One of our tours would be taking us to Capernaum, located on the northern shore of the Sea of Galilee. As soon as I saw the water, I shouted to the driver to stop. In his beautiful accent he said, *"This is not where we stop."* I said, *"Oh, but you have to stop, you must. There's something I need to get."* I begged and pleaded with all my heart and he finally said, *"Ok, I stop...but only for a minute."* I excitedly said, *"Ok, it will only take a minute."*

So he pulled over, I jumped out and ran as fast as I could down to the rocky shoreline, hoping and praying I would find a heart-rock. As soon as I reached the shore I looked down—and there it was—a heart-shaped rock meant just for me. I am certain Jesus placed it tenderly in my path to make this finding extra special. It was February 14th, Valentine's Day. Jesus is and will always be my number one love, my Forever Valentine!

I held it in my hand, caressing it . . . my heart bursting with joy. Then I noticed there was a 'pock' mark—an indentation, right into the center of the rock. I'm certain Jesus left this special stone for me because that 'pock' mark is my reminder of when His truth pierced my heart. Jesus said,

I am the way, the truth and the life.
No one comes to the Father except through me.
John 14:16

You know, we only get one shot in this life here on earth, only one go around. This is not a rehearsal. We can go through this life like the girl *Much-Afraid* with her two companions, Sorrow and Suffering, or we can go to our Perfect Shepherd who promises to be our Rock, our Strength and Comforter. We can hang on to Him, knowing spiritual blessings often come wrapped in trials.

God created us and He knows everything about us. He knows we live in a broken, dark and flawed world and that's why He sent us Jesus.

I get it now! Seeing 'John 3:16' on the graduation cap, so long ago—it was never about my birthday! How foolish I was! Jesus stands at the door of our heart and knocks. He knocked at the door of my heart for many years and waited patiently. Today, I have different 'eyes' to see the world. How could I not praise Him each and every day for what He has done for me? I know what I used to be and what I am today, and I give God all the glory.

As I write this I can tell you I have never been happier in my life than I am today. God gave me a second chance. He blessed me with a wonderful relationship with my husband, Bill, who loves me and our Lord. We have celebrated twenty-five years of marriage and I thank God for second blessings. My tears today are tears of joy and thanksgiving. I know I don't have to be perfect anymore. I'm still a work-in-progress and that's OK, because I know God loves me just the way I am.

~14~

Spiritual Gifts

Each one should use whatever gift he has received to serve others,
faithfully administering God's grace in its various forms.
1 Peter 4:10

After I became a Christian and a member of the church, many people were rejoicing with me and said they were excited to see how God would use the spiritual gifts He had given me. I'm thinking to myself, what are they talking about? What spiritual gifts? I have no gifts, I was certain of that. But the reply was always the same. *"You do have unique God given gifts, Donna, and God will reveal them to you for the glory of God and the good of humanity."*

Oh, ok. I knew I was on a journey and this was new, and I was excited about all the things that were unfolding before me as I was becoming a follower of Christ. I wanted nothing more than to serve Him and to be His servant—a servant with a Shepherd's heart.

As I continued to study the word of God and immerse myself in the Bible, I learned that we all have different gifts, according to the grace given to us. (Romans 12:6). We are all used to build up the church of Christ, and spiritual gifts do this. We are to be a part of the whole body of Christ—to work together for His glory. Each spiritual gift from God is equal to all other gifts; no one is superior to another. (1 Corinthians 13). I was eager to learn and discover more about my spiritual gifts.

After taking a Spiritual Gift Assessment test, I found out that I did, in fact, have gifts. I discovered I had the gifts of mercy, evangelism, faith, and that of being a pastor-teacher. Wow! How exciting to know God is omnipotent and knows everything about us and how we can use the gifts He has given us to do His will.

Mercy is categorized under the 'serving gifts'; to reach out to the lonely and those who suffer physical needs; to have compassion and a cheerful heart as you share the love of Jesus with them.

As far back as I can remember, I have always enjoyed visiting and sharing in conversation with the elderly. Maybe it was because my grandmother lived with my family and me for most of my growing up years and I was blessed with an abundance of aunts and uncles who lived nearby. It seems they always had fun and interesting stories to tell, I guess, because they were older and had more life experiences.

When I was asked to prayerfully consider becoming a Deacon to the Home-bounds, those who cannot attend church for a variety of reasons, I remembered a conversation I had with my mother many years earlier. I asked her why it seemed that all my siblings had been blessed with a gift except for me. She reminded me that I had, indeed, been given a gift—it was the gift of love and compassion for others. I had to admit she was right; I did love people. I had always been outgoing and a people-person, that was for sure. (I've never met a stranger.)

Serving as a deacon to the Home-bounds for over ten years, before moving out of state, gave me the opportunity and privilege of sharing in the joys and challenges of the golden years of these folks. Through this ministry, these special people were connected to the family of God, as he used me to nurture their spiritual growth. And the beautiful thing was, my spiritual growth was nurtured, too.

Many of the elderly who live in communities are without family, friends, or even a church family. Many are lonely and just long to feel the touch of another human. It's that simple. To hold a hand, to give a hug and share the promises we have in the Bible with them gives them hope for their tomorrows. I know this to be true, because I have heard it said to me over and over too many times to count. These gentle people ministered back to me the truth and promise of God's word and faithfulness.

Praise be to the God and Father of our Lord Jesus Christ,
the Father of compassion and the God of all comfort,
who comforts us in all our troubles,
so that we can comfort those in any trouble
with the comfort we ourselves have received from God.
2 Corinthians 1:3-4

My experience with the Home-bounds has been one of great joy, and I feel so blessed that God has called me into this ministry—to have a servant's heart and to be the hands and feet of Christ fills my soul. It's a wonderful gift and an honor to be able to pray with these people and share in communion together. I always left my visits with my cup overflowing, knowing I had extended God's love and hope to them.

It's important to remember there are different spiritual gifts. Some people are not always out in the 'spotlight' for others to see their gifts at work, but often they are working behind the scenes, still working hard, getting the Lord's work done.

I would like to tell you about one such person, an elderly woman who was one of the Home-bounds I had the privilege of ministering to for seven years before she entered into her heavenly mansion at age 93.

Although this woman was not able to attend Sunday services due to a medical condition that kept her bedridden, she was an asset to our church family. The scripture tells us,

Now you are the body of Christ,
and each one of you is a part of it.
1Corinthians 12:27

On one of my visits, I found this woman sitting up in bed, applying labels to what looked to be a box of pamphlets. I asked her what she was doing and she said very modestly, *"Oh, I'm just doing my little job I do each month."* I was surprised to discover it was this woman who put the address labels on our monthly church newsletter, but I was really moved when she told me she said a prayer for each family as she applied the label. Each month that I received my newsletter, I remembered this special lady who said a prayer, not only for me, but for every member in our church. A beautiful example of how God can use each and every one of us to do his will, even if you are bedridden.

After serving as a Deacon to the Home-bounds for more than ten years, I felt God tugging at my heart to get involved with hospital visitations. I enrolled in a six-week training course required by our community hospital and became a pastoral volunteer. Because of my experiences and love for the Home-bounds, praying for their physical needs, giving them hope, strengthening their faith and showing them the compassion of Christ, I felt called to volunteer on the oncology floor.

Of course, anything new and out of our comfort zone can feel a little intimidating, but I know that sometimes God wants to stretch us in areas we may feel like a 'fish out of water', but if we trust in him and follow his lead, it is always glorifying to see and witness his steadfast goodness on those who love and obey him.

For six years I volunteered at our local hospital. Every week that I volunteered, I left that hospital at the end of my shift feeling joy and happiness for doing the Lord's work. As you can imagine, after six years I had said countless prayers, offered my listening ears, held many hands, gave hugs, and shared in their tears. So many visits, each one unique. So many memories. But there are a couple that I will never forget.

I remembered entering a patient's room and found a man crying out to me to please come close and pray for him. He seemed so frightened and anxious. I pulled up a chair, sat at his side, and he reached his hand out. As his hand slid into mine, there was a calmness that came over him and he asked me if I knew Jesus and believed in him. Of course, my answer was a resounding, *"Yes,"* and he said he believed in Him, too, and asked if I would I pray for him. After my prayer, he had a radiant smile on his face and thanked me profusely; he knew he would be with Jesus one day soon.

Shortly a nurse entered the room, and she was shocked to find me sitting so close to the bed and holding this patient's hand. She said, *"Didn't you see the sign?"* I'm thinking, what sign? She pointed above the patient's head and there was a large sign with the words written in big, block letters that said, COMBATIVE PATIENT, APPROACH WITH CAUTION.

Well, I just sat there stunned while this man who was still holding my hand, beamed with delight as a huge smile encompassed his face. Now, anyone who knows me will tell you, I do not take risks, nor would I ever put myself in harm's way. I have common sense, and I always exercise it. But I can tell you this. I never, ever saw that sign over his bed. I believe with all my heart that God knew this man needed to feel his love and grace and for whatever reason, the compassion in my heart outweighed my human vision, and I believe God 'blocked' that sign from my sight so I could do his will for his beloved child. God can do that. He has that kind of power over any given situation. That's how much God loves his children. Every single one of us!

Another visit I will always carry in my heart is proof and evidence of the power of the human touch. Holding a person's hand or giving a pat on the arm can mean a great deal to someone fighting fear and loneliness. As I entered the room of an elderly lady who was dying of cancer, I introduced myself. I offered to pray for her. She told me her pastor had just been there and she was "ok in that department" but could I just please sit down and hold her hand for a while. I said, *"Of course I will"* and I took her hand in mine. She started to cry and said, *"There's just something so powerful about the human touch."* I just sat there, held her hand and we were silent. No words were ever spoken and it was a beautiful experience.

God designed us to be there for one another in this crazy, chaotic world filled with so many uncertainties. He created us to be a community, to love our neighbor as ourself, and in that moment, I was the loving neighbor this woman needed. To feel the touch of another human being is so powerful. God created us to feel the love and comfort of another human being because that's how He designed us to be . . . loving to our neighbor as to ourself.

Scripture says,

Comfort, comfort my people, says your God.

Another gentleman I visited, and will never forget, actually became a member of my church! This was an elderly man who was quite a character. On my initial visit with him, he told me he was raised in Oahu, Hawaii. I told him I lived there as a child when my father was stationed in Kaneohe Bay. He told me he was a surfer and used to surf with the famous Duke

Kahanamoku. I told him I used to surf, and we just hit it off instantly.

He told me he had just lost his wife to Alzheimer's three months earlier and was really missing her and was brokenhearted. I asked if I could pray for him, and he was very open to it. Afterwards, he was trying to hold back his tears. I told him it was OK to cry, that his tears were precious to the Lord and that the shortest verse in the Bible is two words, "Jesus wept." If it was ok for Jesus to cry, well then, he could cry too.

At that, he asked me where I went to church, and I told him. He said, *"When I get out of here and I get better, I'm coming to your church."* Not long after that, one Sunday morning, there he was! Our friendship really began; one that lasted twelve years.

I had the privilege of seeing this great man and funny man just hours before he passed away. That visit would be different from all the others, because he wanted to talk about the heavenly home he was ready to move into. I read him scripture, prayed with him, and anointed him with oil. I told him he was a beloved son of the King. He gave me a kiss, and said good-bye.

I feel so blessed I was given the spiritual gift of 'faith' and 'evangelism'. I love to witness and share my joy with others and tell them what God has done in my life. Through these gifts I am honored to share with others the good news of Jesus and the blessed hope we have in him.

It seems like one thing led to another. and eventually I was asked to attend a Leadership Conference for Stephen Ministry, a ministry that offers one-on-one spiritual care to people who are going through a difficult time. So now I was a Stephen Leader, teaching classes to our church members to become lay ministers. God was still opening my eyes to things I thought I would or could never do. I realized this was 'another' spiritual gift—teaching, and having a Shepherd's heart.

For fourteen years, I was connected to a Women's Bible Study. To grow in my relationship with God with other Christian women has become a top priority for me now. It is an opportunity to encourage and build up one another and to carry each other's burdens. Being anchored in God's word is my spiritual therapy for each week.

When we first moved to Colorado and found a church, I was disappointed to learn that there wasn't a weekly Women's Bible Study. I met with the Pastor and told him of my desire to start one and to lead it. He gave me his blessing and, before too long, that's exactly what I did. I put an announcement in the bulletin and had a meeting at my house. Soon afterwards, I had a nice group of women who wanted to study God's word and grow in the knowledge of our Lord. I led that group there for eight years.

At our first gathering, I gave each lady a heart-rock and shared my 'Reader's Digest' version behind the history of them. There was one lady, Pam, so sweet and precious, who had been battling cancer for several years. She would push through her pain and attend our Bible Studies because they were important to her, and for her to be there as a part of the circle of love for Christ. She knew my love for the Home-bounds and asked if I would go with her to visit her elderly mother who was in an assisted living facility. She told me her mother had a deep faith, and how much she loved Jesus. With my deep love for Jesus, she knew we would be a good fit. So we set the date for a visit.

Her mother was a lovely, kind and gentle soul who exuded the love of Christ and I gave her a heart-rock. As she cradled the rock in her hand, she wanted to know the story behind it. I shared with her what the rocks meant for me, and she loved hearing my story. We read scripture, we talked about God's goodness and we prayed, praising Him and giving Him glory for being the loving God that yearns to love and care for his children, no matter what age we are, for we are all precious in His sight.

Sadly, a year after that visit, she was called to her heavenly home, and I was asked by her family to speak at her Memorial Service. Another request was that I would give each great-grandchild a heart-rock as a reminder of how much their great-grandmother loved the Lord. Of course, I was honored to do this.

I gathered up several heart-rocks and wrote Psalm 18:2 on them. I placed them in a beautiful heart-shaped wooden bowl. At the service, after I had spoken, I invited all the great-grandchildren to come forward to pick out a heart-rock. I told them their special rock would not only be a reminder of God's love, but also of the deep love their sweet great-granny had for each of them!

Three years later, Pam, who I mentioned above, was facing another surgery for her cancer. By this time, we had moved back to California, but the church contacted me when she went on hospice, and asked if I would call and pray with her. Of course I would do that for this precious woman!

What an emotional and heart-wrenching phone call that was for me, but I knew Jesus would be in our midst and the Holy Spirit would equip me with all that I needed to say. In her weakened voice, she wanted to talk about heaven, because she knew she would be going there soon. We talked about our precious Shepherd, Jesus, who would be walking with her. I read scripture to her and then I prayed a prayer that would be my last for her. She was at peace and knew she would be going home soon, to her 'real home'.

It wasn't long after that phone call that she lost her fight to cancer. I can say she was truly a Christian soldier marching off each day to fight the battle. She didn't look back, but looked forward and fought the fight with grace, and pressed on toward the goal for the prize of the upward call of God in Jesus Christ.

I am forever grateful to God that He continues to use me as His instrument to bring hope and comfort to others. Whatever I give and do in His name, He blesses me back tenfold! I am so honored to be a disciple of Jesus!

When I look back on my life before I became a Christian, I honestly cannot believe the things I am doing today. God is faithful and His love for us is steadfast. When we choose to pick up our cross and follow Him, we will reap a harvest that will glorify God.

Be open to wanting to discover and explore what your spiritual gifts might be and then see how God will use you to further His kingdom here on earth. God created each of us for a purpose, a purpose that will honor, adore and praise His Holy name. That's how much He loves you!

I found this rock outside Max Lucado's church in Texas. Max is my favorite Christian author, and I wanted to meet him to give him a heart-rock. But then, as I was leaving, I spotted this rock out by the parking lot.

As you can see, it's not the typical heart shaped rock, but rather, the heart seems to be embossed into it.

~15~

A Few More Rock Stories

When we learned about the mass on Bill's kidney, we were trying not to worry too much about the situation until we had met with the doctor at the City of Hope on Friday, March 8, 2013. Instead we focused on God and His love for us, knowing that whatever the outcome might be, we wouldn't go through it alone, Jesus would be with us every step of the way.

Surgery was set for mid-April, and we were allowed to go back to Colorado to get things in order before returning. But before doing that, we had people to see and things to do, one of which was going to our church in Mission Viejo. It was a Sunday that I will not forget.

The church was doing a series on 'prayer' and I was only sorry I couldn't attend to hear all of the sermons, because prayer is one of my biggest passions. There was a guest singer that day, and she sang a solo about prayer.

I was mesmerized by her voice, her joy and her spirit, for the way she delivered that song gave glory to the Lord. She was belting it out! It had been less than forty-eight hours since we learned Bill would be having surgery for kidney cancer, and all I could do was think about how many prayers we would be depending on in the coming month. I couldn't hold the tears back; they just came and came. I knew it was God's plan that we would be in church that Sunday to hear this amazing woman sing. Every note that came out of her mouth sank down into the depths of my soul and I knew, after the service, I would be meeting this woman, and she would become my new friend.

After the postlude, I ran up to the choir room, still sobbing, and found her. Through my tears, I introduced myself and told her how much that song spoke to my heart. I shared with her about Bill's upcoming surgery at City of Hope and asked if she would pray for him. She told me she worked at Azusa Pacific University, which was just down the road from City of Hope. She said she would not only pray for Bill, but she would COME to the hospital and pray with him before surgery!

We exchanged phone numbers so we could stay in touch, and she gave me her business card. That's when I learned she was an Adjunct Voice Instructor, Gospel Choir Director and Vocal Instructor at the University! Well no wonder that girl could sing like Aretha Franklin! What a gifted, exceptional, and accomplished singer she was. Her name was Letitia Ugweke.

We came back a month later for the surgery. I contacted Letitia to keep her updated on our schedule. As the date for surgery drew near, Letitia's schedule at the university didn't coordinate with ours and it was clear she wouldn't be able to come to the hospital and pray over Bill prior to his surgery.

But God is good! Bill and I were staying in a hotel near the City of Hope to make the commute a lot easier than driving through traffic from Orange County. Letitia surprised us when she came to our hotel room to spend the evening with us and to give that prayer as promised. How nice it was to spend one-on-one time with this godly woman who gave of her time for us, her two new friends. To be in prayer, in that hotel room, just the three of us, brought such joy and gladness, knowing God's tender mercies and goodness would supply our every need as we prepared for the early morning surgery the next day.

'Life' is what happens when you're making other plans. At the last minute, before Bill was to be wheeled into the operating room, the surgery was canceled. More testing was needed, and the surgery was postponed for ten days. The silver lining was that we now had extra days to visit with family and friends, and that included our new friend, Letitia.

I contacted Letitia to let her know the surgery had been postponed for ten days. She said, *"Well then, how would you and Bill like to come to the university and sit in for one of the gospel choir rehearsals? We're going to be performing the following week in the Munson Chapel Hall on campus and I'd like it very much if the both of you would come."* The response was a very speedy, *"Yes, absolutely yes!"*

We met Letitia in her office where she told us all about what she did with the gospel choir, and then she showed us around campus. I took a special heart-rock along and gave it to her. (She told me recently that she still carries it in her book bag for class each day.)

How exciting it was to be in that rehearsal room . . . to hear these young adults . . . shining their lights and singing their hearts out for Christ. Their body movements as they sang, the joy radiating from them—it was so spectacular to witness and hear. I just wanted to grab a tambourine and start dancing for the Lord, that's how over the top these kids were, and this was just a rehearsal. We looked forward to that concert that took place the night before Bill's surgery.

Munson Chapel was small, beautiful, and intimate. We settled into our seats and chose to sit towards the back, leaving the seats closer to the front for family and friends of this extraordinary choir. What a blessing it was to be invited to this uplifting concert, but soon a bigger blessing was to come.

After the last song was sung and the applause quieted down, Letitia thanked everyone for coming. Then she said, *"Tonight, I have two new friends here with us.* (My heart skipped a beat.) *Their names are Bill and Donna. I met them last month at their church in Mission Viejo when I was a guest singer. Now they are back again because Bill will be having kidney surgery tomorrow morning at the City of Hope. I would like to invite Bill and Donna to please come up to the chancel area so we can lay hands on them and lift them up in prayer."* Well, here came the tears again as I was moved by their compassion for us.

We worked our way up to the chancel area, and then these beautiful spirit-filled young adults, who had just ministered to my heart and soul to overflowing, encircled Bill and me, placed their hands upon us and prayed, prayed, prayed and then prayed some more. I was overwhelmed, overjoyed and grateful to each of them for showing the love of Christ to us through their beautiful prayers. It was comforting to know we had a cloud of prayer that would hover over us and be with us the next morning and in the days to follow as Bill recovered. I praise God for all the ways He fills up my emptiness with His fullness. To Him be the Glory!

Bill's surgery was successful. The mass, fortunately, was contained and completely removed.

A lovely Christian couple, Lyle and Betty Johnson, from our church in Mission Viejo, offered for us to stay at their home while Bill recovered before we could make our drive back to Colorado. We were so grateful for their hospitality and love for us.

I found a large lovely rock from a huge mound that is piled high outside the parking lot at the City of Hope and I placed it outside the Johnson's front yard for all to see. The rock symbolized to me that their house, this beautiful sanctuary for us to stay in, was a house of hope!

After deciding to purchase a home in Arizona, we knew we would be embarking on another adventure and, most importantly, we knew God would be with us. We would be making drives out to check on the progress of our home, to find a church, which was hugely important, and to explore around the town to meet new people—people God would be bringing into our lives to become our new friends and neighbors.

In early January of 2018, as we made a trip out (which would result in the purchase of our lot), we spotted a very interesting place we had never really noticed before. Maybe because we were now going to be residents of Arizona, we were paying more attention, checking things out and taking it all in.

Driving from California on Highway 89, at an elevation of four thousand feet, you go through a little town called Yarnell. This is the town where the nineteen firefighters, the Granite Mountain 'Hot Shots', were tragically killed in the 2013 fire.

After you reach the top of that mountain, there is a very unique and fascinating shop. We had never noticed it on the right hand side, but this time it really caught our eye, and we decided to stop to check it out. It was called Sunrise Mining.

The property was filled with beautiful pieces of carved stone benches, tables, and the biggest water feature we had ever seen—a pristine piece of marble or travertine stone about nine feet tall, with water cascading down from the top, hitting and bouncing off just the right spots of stone as the water made its way down to the bottom. It was stunning to see and awesome to listen to. It was truly a sight to behold.

We were intrigued and wanted to learn more about this shop and meet the person behind it, but unfortunately it was closed. We decided we would stop by on our way back to California but, again, it was closed. There was a sign on the door that said, 'At the mines.' We peeked through the window and couldn't believe all the interesting things inside that had to do with mining. It looked like a museum. Bill wrote down the phone number so we could be in touch on the next drive out.

It was only two weeks later that we had an appointment with the Design Center to select the items for our home. However, Bill would not be able to go, as he was coaching high school Track and Field, so it was up to me to drive. I brought my girlfriend, Judith Hoel, who was also our designer, to help me with the appointment. What a fun road trip we had.

During that drive, we were halfway across the desert when my phone rang and the caller I.D. said, Pete the Miner. I'm thinking who is Pete the Miner? Well, Bill had made contact with Sunrise Mining and Pete was the owner; Bill had given him my phone number. I put the call on 'speaker' so Judith could hear the conversation, too. He was so friendly and personable, so easy to talk to, and after five minutes you felt like you had known him your whole life.

I told him my husband and I had stopped by a week ago, but the shop was closed and now I was driving out again with a friend and I was hoping the shop would be open. No such luck. Pete told me he was down in Scottsdale at an art show. I mentioned the incredibly beautiful water feature we had seen and he said he was hoping to sell it that weekend.

182

During that phone conversation Pete asked us if we had ever watched the TV show, 'Extreme Makeover', the show on ABC where the community comes together and remodels a home for someone. Then, for the reveal, they bring in a big bus, park it in front of the home, and shout, 'Move that bus, Move that bus.'

We both said, *"Of course, we remember that show and we loved it."*

"Well," Pete says, *"I was on that show for eight seasons. I was the 'rock artist' and did the water features and other artsy stuff that involved working with different types of stones."*

Wow, now we were talking with a celebrity and it just made the drive across the desert so much more fun. I told Pete we were looking forward to meeting him someday on one of or next trips out and that we had purchased a home in Prescott.

Now that we knew for sure we would be moving, we needed to get creative with the upcoming expense that's involved with a major move. Moving companies charge by the weight, which meant we needed to lighten the load. Rocks are very heavy when you have several hundreds or thousands, and all we could see were dollar signs. So next on the list was to find a storage unit in Prescott and take all my heart-rocks there.

It was in mid-April that Bill and I loaded up both of our cars with rocks, rocks and more rocks. Every nook and cranny was filled with rocks! This would be a quick turnaround trip—we would spend the night and then drive back to California the next day.

We couldn't wait to start the drive up the mountain, hoping the Sunrise Mining shop would be open. As we rounded the last bend that would bring us to the top, I was anxiously hoping we would get to meet this Pete the Miner. The shop came into view and we saw a man driving a huge piece of equipment that had some kind of vice on it that had in its grip a massive slab of marble. We parked our cars and walked towards this man, who stopped the engine and crawled down from whatever that giant tractor was.

It was Pete the Miner and he was even wearing a miner's hat. He looked like he had just walked out of a mine shaft. What a character he was, and so darn friendly. He took us on a personal tour of his shop and showed us everything that had to do with what he makes—hand carved stone. Everything is done by hand and with hand tools. There was an array of beautiful pieces of stone throughout his property, along with historic mining artifacts. He told us he loved rocks and that he had been a miner his whole life.

I told him I also have a love for rocks, rocks that are shaped like hearts. I gave him the 'Reader's Digest' version of my story. I told him we were on our way to a storage unit and then led him over to my car where I popped the trunk for him to check out my rocks. There was a large heart-rock near the front of the trunk and he pointed to it immediately, and said, *"Now that's a real beauty."* And it was.

For whatever reason, he felt comfortable in sharing with us that he had been battling prostate cancer for the past five years and now it was back again and he was undergoing radiation treatments. We told him we were sorry to hear that and we would keep him in our prayers.

We chatted for a while more and then told him once our house was finished and we were settled in, we would like to talk to him about a small water feature for our backyard. We said our good-byes as we needed to get back on the road so we could get to the storage unit to unload my rocks from both cars before it got dark.

When we were back on the road, I was replaying in my mind all that we had just seen at Sunrise Mining, and to finally meet in person, Pete the Miner. I couldn't stop thinking about his having to fight cancer a second time, and then it hit me: why on earth didn't I give him that heart-rock? He said it was a beauty and it would have been the perfect reminder of God's love for him during his second battle with cancer. I decided right then and there I would give Pete that rock when we would be driving back through town the next morning.

We got on the road early and when we arrived at Pete's shop we found it was closed! Luckily, I had his phone number and called. He said he wasn't open because he was feeling too tired from the radiation treatments he had been receiving and was going to take it easy that day.

I told him I wanted to give him the heart-rock he liked so much and that I was sorry I hadn't given it to him on the spot. He told me to leave the rock at the front door; it would be safe there, and he would get it later. I told him, *"This heart-rock will be your reminder that God loves you and you are not alone on this journey. God will be with you every step of the way and,, whatever you're facing, He will face it with you. He will be your Rock, your Strength and your Refuge. Remember God loves you and I'll be praying for you."* In a strong and positive voice he replied, *"10-4!"* 10-4 means, Ok, understood, and affirmative. Yay, I think I got the message across!

Pete the Miner is now another friend. After moving into our house, we made a trip out to his shop where we walked around the property and picked out a perfect piece of stone for a water feature for our backyard. We look forward to having this special feature to be a part of our landscape. Now, whenever I call Pete the Miner he answers by saying, *"Hi, heart-rock lady"* and when the conversation is over, he ends it with not good-bye, but *10-4!* Ok, understood and affirmative.

We still make trips back to California to see family and friends, and Pete the Miner is one of the stops we make along the way. His large 'beauty' of a heart-rock is displayed in his office, so he sees it every day, a daily reminder.

God loves him and is with him always. And I'm pretty sure Pete knows it, too.

10-4

After we moved to Prescott and were renting a cabin until our house was completed, we made an appointment to meet with the person who would be doing our landscaping at the house. His name was Nathan Hannah, the owner of Rock'n'Earth Landscaping.

Now, I'm thinking, with a company name like that, this guy needs to have a heart-rock, so when we met him, I gave him one. It's just so much fun to do—to extend God's love through a heart-rock. And who wouldn't want one? They're awesome! He loved it, and I shared my faith and how it all came about. After a short conversation, I knew that he, too, was a Christian.

He asked if this would be our last move. *"Yes"*, we said. His reply was, *"Everyone says that, but then they end up moving again."* I told him this would be our last move here on earth, and the next move would be when we moved up to glory, to heaven.

On one of his phone calls, I remember his asking me how many heart-rocks I had . . . ten, twenty? I told him, *"I have hundreds, if not thousands!"* He was astounded and said the reason he was asking was that he wanted to incorporate some of them into our landscape. Wow, what a great idea; I loved it.

He asked if we would bring some of my heart-rocks over to his nursery. He wanted to err on the side of safety and said his plan would be to attach (with some kind of adhesive) some of my heart-rocks onto pieces of flagstone, so that in the case we ever wanted to move again, it would be easily available to pick up and take with us. How clever is that?

So we loaded up the car with wire baskets of all shapes and sizes of my heart-rocks and delivered them to his nursery. He said he would make the selections and just surprise us. And surprise us he did! We have a very beautiful pathway in our backyard that just screams out the love and creation of Christ. And the added bonus is that we have a custom fire pit that has the seventeen pound heart-rock from Sitka, Alaska, set in the stone on the top ring!

Next Nathan wanted to know if I had any large, big heart-rocks and I told him of course I did. I have rocks in all shapes AND sizes. He went on to tell me his next idea for our front yard. The way the land was graded, he would build a retaining wall that would face the house. His plan was to incorporate three very large heart-rocks, equally spaced out, within the retaining wall. I said, *"I love the idea of three heart-rocks, and you know what it will represent?"* At that moment, we both said in unison, *"The Trinity: Father, Son and Holy Spirit!"* Because it faces the front of the house, anyone who is sitting on the front porch, or guests who are in the front guestrooms, will be able to see this beautiful work of art.

So now there is a driveway in Littleton, Colorado, that has a heart-rock imbedded in it, and in Prescott, Arizona, a fire pit with a seventeen-pound heart-rock on the top. I am reminded of the scripture from Isaiah 28:16.

Therefore says the Lord God,
"Behold, I am the one who has laid as a foundation in Zion,
a stone, a tested stone, a precious cornerstone, of a sure
foundation."

We were so blessed to have our new home stamped with the love and power of God for all to see! To top it off, we discovered our home is situated on a heart-shaped street. Our house is right at the top of the 'heart', just like Christ is at the top of mine!

Now that we have this beautiful desert landscaping, how do we care for it, considering that we're from Southern California? We decided to hire the company who did our landscaping, 'Rock n Earth', to maintain our yard each month, with their expertise care.

On the first day the landscapers arrived, there were two men, one quite young looking and the other older. They asked what kind of look were we wanting for our landscaping, 'manicured' or 'wild' looking? I screamed neither! I don't want a manicured Japanese garden in Arizona, nor do I want a jungle. I want 'natural' looking.

The older of the two went over to our big beautiful pots that held the evergreen plants, Boxwoods and said, *"Now we won't cut these back severely, but we will prune them back just enough that they will produce more."* Excitedly I said, *"Yes, just like in the Bible, John 15, where Jesus says, 'Every branch in Me that does not bear fruit, He takes away, and every branch that bears fruit He prunes, that it may bear more fruit.'* At that, the younger man, Michael Ketner, responded by saying, *"Wow, I like that!"*

So I go on and on, saying that if we abide in Jesus, we bear much fruit, but without Him we are nothing. Michael then asked if we went to church and if so, what one. I told him, of course! We found a church the day after we bought our lot. He said he didn't really go to church because of the politics and all, but he believed in God and said he goes to the woods and he knows God is there, so that is his church.

I responded by saying, *"Yes, that is so true. God IS there in the woods. He's there in the mountains, the desert, in the oceans; God is everywhere, because God is Omnipotent; He has unlimited power and His presence is everywhere. However, there is something about being in church, in the house of the Lord, standing on holy ground. Jesus tells us in scripture we are to worship with one another, and that is how we deepen our faith."*

There are many scriptures that command us to go to church. Connecting with other believers helps us to grow our faith more deeply, to stay anchored in God's word. It helps us to be accountable and to be there for one another, to encourage and lift up. It's not complicated to figure out. Without weekly worship, we can fall off track and drift away. When you build a fire, to keep it going, you must add coals. In much the same way, to keep your faith fired up, you must stoke your heart with other believers and find a place to worship.

I told Michael that he will not find a perfect church anywhere because we live in a broken world, but we worship and praise our Father in heaven, and we go to church to pray together and sing Him praises. There is truly something that pierces your soul when you are in the house of the Lord on a Sunday!

When my landscapers moved to the backyard, I showed them the awesome heart-rock vignettes and told them my faith story. I showed them one of my prized rocks I found in Colorado that has two red stripes going across it . . . the reminder that by His stripes we are healed. Michael said, *"That just gave me the chills."* I have a gabion on our patio that houses many heart-rocks and I told each of them to feel free to take one when they left, a reminder of God's love for them.

I came back into the house and left them alone to do what gardeners do—water, fertilize and trim back shrubs. Later the doorbell rang and I opened the door to find Michael standing there. I asked him where his partner was, and he said he was down the street working on another yard. In a very heartfelt and humble voice, he said, *"I just want to thank you for what you have said to me today"* Michael became very emotional and said, *"I really needed to hear it and I know God wanted me to be here today."* The tears were coming and I wrapped my arms around him, gave him a kiss on the cheek and said, *"Oh, it's ok, God loves you and He knows all about you."*

God is the 'Master Weaver' and He knows where we need to be to feel His love and power and on that day, God used me to share love and hope into this young man's heart. I was paying it forward, for all God has done for me. God's the Weaver, and we are the threads.

On one of our trips back to Colorado, we were blessed when we stopped for lunch at a Cracker Barrel in Gallup, New Mexico. Our food server was a young man who was very personable. He asked where we were coming from and where did we live. We told him we would be passing through again in a few weeks and told him about Bill's upcoming surgery. I gave him a heart-rock (I always seem to have them with me) and he was so happy to get it. He told us he was a Christian and loved Jesus.

When he brought us our food he said, *"Guess what? One of our Deacons is here for dinner on the other side, and I would love to bring her over so the both of us can pray over Bill, if that would be ok with you."*

"Ok? Of course! Go and get her," I said. The food server introduced us to the Deacon, and they both placed hands upon my husband and said the most beautiful prayer, right there in Cracker Barrel.

On our drive out for the surgery, we stopped at that same Cracker Barrel, hoping to see this young man who had blessed us that day, but he no longer worked there. I even called the church where he said he attended; no one ever answered the phone and there was no voice message I could leave. We never saw him again and I often wonder if he was an angel God had placed in our path that day.

* * * * *

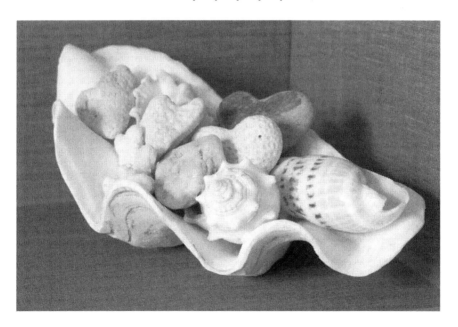

* * * * *

* * * * *

* * * * *

Conclusion

I stand at the door and knock.
If anyone hears my voice and opens the door,
I will come in and eat with him, and he with me.
Revelation 3:20

If you do not know Jesus and have not embraced Him as your Lord and Savior, it is my prayer that through my story and what He has done for me in my life, you will be inspired to seek Him with all your heart.

Maybe you have questions about Jesus. Maybe you're not sure He's who He says He is. Let me tell you this: Jesus is not make-believe. This is not a fairy tale. Jesus is the real deal, and He longs for you to know him, to seek Him, to trust in Him and bond your heart with His. You have nothing to lose and everything to gain. You will spend your eternal future with Him in a place of glorious celebration. I know if I were to die today, I will step into my eternal home in heaven.

Jesus is standing at the door of your heart right now and he longs for you to open the door and believe in Him. Do you hear the knock? Jesus is waiting for you.

Jesus wants you to have the gift of eternal life through Him as your Lord and Savior. But He will not force or push himself on you because He is not that kind of God. Jesus is not rude. Jesus is polite, loving, kind, tender and merciful. The choice is yours.

Follow Jesus, seek Him and love Him, for He is the only way. In God's perfect timing, may you come to know Him, as I did.

I would like to close by saying that if you are reading this today and feeling like *Much-Afraid,* not knowing which way to turn, don't give up. Turn to Jesus, your Loving Shepherd. He's listening right this very moment and He hears you. Jesus knows your voice. Jesus knows every hair on your head and every tear you have shed. Your Shepherd has come to restore your soul and He longs to take you to the high places.

May the Shepherd who understands you perfectly and loves you eternally bless you always!

* * * * *

Made in the USA
San Bernardino, CA
12 August 2019